TRANSLATIONS FROM THE SOUL

Advanced Praise for Translations from the Soul

"Ashley helps us dance in the rain with the profound exploration of her poetry. Impactful, inclusive and empowering. Her works are medicine for future exploration, taking us on a journey to deeper understanding. Her words are the destination."

- K8e Orr

"Colorado Springs is blessed by Ashley's vision as a poet and her leadership as poet laureate. May the words in this book not only soothe our weary hearts, but also serve as a compass to guide us into the future of our dreams, a future made possible by visionaries such as herself."

- Nico Wilkinson

"Ashley's poetry, her presence, and her impact on the community in Colorado Springs has been profound. She breathes life into art wherever she goes. She gathers artists, creates space and opportunities for them to flourish. Her poetry is always profound. I can't wait to see what she does next."

- Michael "Skillzilla" Ferguson

"The Universe and beyond, inconceivable. The Earth within it, improbable. Life and humanity from space dust. Incogitable. But Ashley,… Ashley Cornelius; how she exists, what she creates, the ways she inspires us to feel and be, absolutely impossible."

- Matt Block

"Being a poet is not for the faint of heart, and Ashley Cornelius is the truest poet there ever was, but she is so much more - she is a revolutionary! With pen and voice she challenges systems of oppression, strengthens movements, teaches to the masses, gets people thinking and feeling, and reflects a light we all can see ourselves a part of and want to do right by, for ourselves and the world! She is a powerful stand for collective liberation. Ashley creates impact and changes lives with her artistry. We are so lucky to be here at this time as she shares these gifts so generously, inviting us in to pause, listen, learn, heal, and take action."

- Amber Cotè

TRANSLATIONS FROM THE SOUL

ASHLEY CORNELIUS

Wordbinders Publishing
Colorado, USA

Wordbinders Publishing
An imprint of Journey Institute Press,
a division of 50 in 52 Journey, Inc.
journeyinstitutepress.org

Library of Congress Control Number: 2024936669
Names: Cornelius, Ashley
Title: TRANSLATIONS FROM THE SOUL
Description: Colorado: Wordbinders Publishing, 2024
Identifiers: ISBN 979-8-9894379-3-1 (hardcover)
978-1-964754-38-3 (paperback)
978-1-964754-39-0 (ebook/kindle)
Subjects: BISAC:
POETRY / American / African American & Black |
POETRY / LGBTQ+ |
POETRY / Women Authors

First Edition
Printed in the United States of America

1 3 4 5 22 37 43 67 89 99

This book was typeset in Garamond / TW Can MT Condense
Editing by Jessica Medberry, InkWhale Editorial LLC.
Design by WiggleB Studios

CONTENTS

PART 2

This book is dedicated

To my parents, Tammy and John Micheal, for their unwavering love and support. Thank you for cheering me on when I quit my job to become a full-time artist. With special love to my mom who has always believed in me and told me I would achieve incredible things.

To my partner, Chris, for being the best cheerleader and lighthouse I could ask for. Thank you for our basement open mics and dramatic readings that strengthened my poetry and love for the arts.

To Black girls and women who have ever felt the unparalleled greatness within them and dared to let their brilliance shine.

PREFACE

What is poetry? I've often said poetry is anything you put meaning behind. Poetry is how I make meaning of the world and my soul. I consider myself a translator, taking big concepts, emotions, and experiences and making them accessible. As a Black queer woman, I've been able to share the beauty and the hardship of my lived experience through my work. I noticed when I performed my poetry, people listened, and I knew if I have the ability to be heard I wanted to speak about advocacy, activism, anti-racism, and revolutionary joy. My journey began with translating my own experiences and opening up my heart in the form of words. It has now led me to the position of Pikes Peak Region Poet Laureate, where my translation is harnessed as a community gift. This book is a compilation of complex emotions and experiences translated into poems. The first part contains poems I wrote for myself; the poems in the second part were commissioned by community members and leaders. You'll find some of the poems have stories about my inspiration and motivation to provide a closer look at my creative process. I'm excited for you to learn my language and how I care for myself and others.

PART 1

Poetry is a conversation with yourself. Poems can reveal truths, joy, pain, and emotions you didn't realize you were holding. I invite you to read the ways poetry has been a gift to my soul and an outlet for my experiences.

During a trip to Meow Wolf in Santa Fe, New Mexico, I saw a sticker on a stop sign that said "Commit Poetry." This phrase deeply resonated with my experiences as a Black woman. Our society, as a result of White Supremacy, has criminalized Blackness. Getting followed in stores, questioning my presence at certain events, or pulled over by police are common experiences. The assumption for Black people is guilty until proven innocent. I had a revelation that if society thinks I'm going to commit a crime, then I'm going to commit my poetry. I'm going to dedicate myself to my art. This poem is an extended metaphor, one of my favorite literary devices.

Commit Poetry

Expose your inner thoughts to willing participants.
Burn down the stage and leave it smoldering.
Let the ashes of your words permeate the space.
You will be the main suspect in a series of fires. Your arson tongue has no plans of stopping.
Snatch attention and edges. Steal gasps.
Rob the audience of their misinformation. Replace it with your premeditated experiences.
Murder the mic. Bury the body in the back of your mind with the rest of your trauma.
Do not go quietly. Scream not guilty, with your fingers crossed behind your back
Aggravate society with the assault of your sound.
Arm yourself with literary devices.
Shotgun similes and musket metaphors.
Drop symbolism bombs.
Throw tear gas vulnerability.
Use your sharp lines to cut a bitch.
Throw your fist in the air as a warning shot.

Distribute your voice like dime bags.
Be the plug.
Get high on your own supply.
Know the value of your product, the way it makes the consumer feel when they snort each line. Your shit is pure.
Take the money and skip town.
Wash it clean.
Launder it out to dry and use it to buy back your hostage voice.
Pay off your insecurities. Assume a new identity, cut your hair, change your name.
Walk with the confidence of a mediocre White man.
Hustle your speech.
Disturb the peace.
Incite vernacular revolution.
Riot in-between the lines on your sheets.
Picket with your pen.
Fuck the policing of expression.
Resist silence.
Vandalize our history books and rewrite the narratives.
Break the sound system.
Commit Poetry.

The Poem Is an Invitation

This poem requires nothing from you.
You have no tasks. No responsibilities.
You answer only to your mind, body, and spirit.
Lean into this connection.
Adjust your body, tend to your needs, and be held by this poem.

Tune into the unique rhythm of your breath. Your body is a full orchestra.
Take time to learn how your breath adds to the beauty of your body's sound.
Breathe deeply.
Every inhale is the filling of your body with what you need.
Each exhale is a letting go of things that do not serve you.
Stay here.
Breathe and give life to what is needed and blow out what is not.

This poem belongs to you. These affirmations are intrinsically true. Take what you need. Take more than what you need. You deserve abundance. You deserve a cup that overflows.

I know these things to be true.
You are enough.
You are valid.

You are exceptional.
You are made from decades of survival and resilience.
You are worthy of rest.
You are strong.
Your productivity does not determine your worth.
You get to be tired.
Your emotions are valid.
Your self-care is necessary.
There are systems literally created to oppress you, and you have survived.
Give yourself permission to mourn, to grieve, to heal, to honor what you need.

We sit in one of the most difficult times in our lives.
We are the ancestors.
We are finding survival and hope in each other.
There are tears, loss, and pain, and we hold space for beauty, creation, and joy.

This is an invitation to lower your shoulders and put down what you've been carrying.
Let this poem hold it for a while.
This is an invitation to unclench your jaw.
Welcome the release.
Softening of muscle and spirit.

If your mind wanders or you believe you are not worthy of these affirmations.
If you think you should not accept this invitation, smile.
Know this poem is a bountiful harvest and you can collect all that belongs to you.

Your joy is necessary.
Your rest is revolutionary.
Taking care of yourself is a priority.

Your existence in this world is crucial.
There is possibility and abundance in your future.
You are rising to the apex of your success.
Lean into the transition to new life and opportunity.

Return to your breath.
Connect your hand with your stomach or chest.
Feel the rise and fall of your body.
Stay here as long as you need.
Your breath is always available to you.

This is an invitation to open your eyes, adjust your body, to walk away full and nourished.
Remember your body is a full orchestra; Every breath adds to the unique beauty of your body's sound.
This poem is always here, is always true, and it is completely yours.

Black culture and entertainment drive American culture. The way "out" of one's neighborhood or socioeconomic status is usually through a form or performance like sports, music, or dance. After getting mistaken for a singer over and over again, I began playing with the idea of meeting the expectations of society as a Black woman with a talent to behold.

Right?

I look like I can sing, right?
Got that Aretha Franklin, Chaka Khan kinda vibes, right?
I look like my throat is full of negro spirituals, right?
Could lead enslaved people to safety with this voice, right?
Hit the high note, hand on the ear like Mariah, right?
Body big like a church choir director, right?
Soulful, smooth, satin-lined songs, right?

I mean I must be some type of musical, right?
If not a song, then I look like I can dance, right?
Black beauty with thick thighs clapn' in a music video, right?
Twerk something in the club with my girls, right?
Dirty whine like Rihanna in Barbados, right?
Pop it on the pole for the men who will pay, right?

Right?
Because this body must be entertainment, right?
Has to be sellable to the massas I mean masses, right?
Gotta be sexy, right?

Soulful, right?
Easy, right?
Thick right?
Down, right?
Ain't no use for a Black girl if she ain't talented, right?
So I got to look like I got soul, right?
Look like I've been to war in this world, right?
Body brown so they know I had it hard, right?
Light enough so they ain't scared, right?
Big body so they know I can carry my weight, right?
4c hair so they know I'm authentic, right?
Gold chains so they know I can be chained, right?

But at least I look like I can sing, right?
Look like I can dance, right?
Look like something you might like, right?

Eviction Notice

I am not afraid to be queer.
I am afraid of how easily hate makes its home in this town as if it is a welcome guest.
My queerness is a hostile eviction notice.

Dislodged

My queerness has been stuck between my teeth for as long as I can remember.

I would feel it, know it was always there.

Sometimes I fantasized about what it might feel like to dislodge the truth and roll it around in my mouth, to say the words and make a home for it, give it a name, and share it with others.

But for so long, it stayed a secret in the back of my mouth.

I found spaces where it felt like everyone had found a way to pick at the truth and was vibrantly existing with this new freedom.

I don't think I could have found my way to the words, to the coming forward and out, without first existing in and engaging with poetry, writing, and queerness.

The catalyst was the mutual acceptance of queerness within my relationship.

The safety I felt with them allowed me to dislodge queer from my teeth and let it reveal itself as pansexual.
It enveloped my mouth like velvet, ran down my throat like

chamomile tea, and warmed the parts of me I didn't realize were freezing.

To the Parents Who Pray Their Child Isn't Gay

Pray your child is healthy.
Pray they have universal healthcare.
Pray they are well-adjusted.
Pray they eat their boogers in private and are kind to animals.
Pray they fall in love with themselves.
Never become abusive partners.
Do not experience sexual assault
Pray their names aren't remembered as a headline.
Pray they do not become a martyr to a movement that will
write their eulogy in hashtags.
Pray they will always have clean drinking water.
Pray they will never flow into the birth-to-prison pipeline, or
pray pipelines will never run through their heritage.
Pray they are funny and can laugh at themselves.
Pray they know the power of their voice.
Pray they have a best friend.
Are creative and never lose their imagination.
Know that heartbreak leads to love.
Learn the stars are a reminder of ancestral legacies.
Pray they have rights they'll talk about for years.
Feel the vibrations of bodies dancing in unison at concerts.
Pray they appreciate the way music jump-starts hearts.
Lean into the sweet embrace of nostalgia.
Ask that they learn how to forgive themselves.
Seek help when they need it,

Pray they find a partner who buys them tacos and likes their butt.
Pray they find their passion.
Know the rush of sneaking dessert in the middle of the night.
Pray they are safe.

If they are gay, pray they see you as a soft landing.
Come out knowing there is love on the other side.
Do not seek death as the answer to ending pain.
Pray they live every moment fully.
Welcome them into your home again and again and again.
Remind them they will always be your child.
Support them when the world is cruel.
Pray they bury you first.
Pray your child never has to wonder if the only thing you prayed for was for them not to be gay.

Black leaders' advocacy and revolutionary acts have directly impacted civil and human rights. To take it a step further, securing these rights has resulted directly from the work of Black queer people. Yet, Black queer people continue to be discriminated against and discredited. The history of human rights is full of Black queer voices, and this poem features a small fraction of the legacy and power of Black queer lives!

Black Queer Lives Matter

When you say Black Lives Matter, remember, you are speaking into existence the labor and dedication of Black and queer women.
Alicia Garza, Patrisse Cullors, and Ayo Tometi planted and watered the roots of this movement.

When you recite "I Have a Dream," you are channeling the work and linguistics of a Black gay man, Bayard Rustin, adviser to Dr. Martin Luther King Jr.
The same man who was jailed and threatened for his sexual orientation and forced to remain behind the limelight next to Dr. King.

When you attend Pride, acknowledge you are standing on the bricks and mortar of a Black trans woman, Marsha "Pay it no mind" Johnson, who was instrumental in the Stonewall riot. All while providing support to unhoused queer youth and sex workers in Manhattan.

When you call for this movement to be intersectional, remember you are honoring the work of a Black queer woman, Audre Lorde, self-identified "Black, lesbian, feminist, mother, poet, warrior." Paving the way for women to reclaim their eroticism, their bodies, and their voices.

When you demand "No justice, no peace," recognize this is a prayer for all the Black trans women who are missing and murdered.

When you raise your fist, it is in solidarity with the pursuit of joy and rest for Black queer youth navigating oppressive systems.

When you yell ACAB, make sure you understand you are fighting against the panic defense, which justifies the assault and murder of queer folks based on their identities.

When you protest in the streets, know this movement is queer
Is nonbinary
Is trans
Is Black
Realize, we walk in the footsteps of Black queer leaders who dedicated their lives so that we can continue to say Black Lives Matter.

Communal Grief

My intersectionalities take turns grieving each other.
I do not know a time when they are not in mourning.

The Club Q shooting adds to the list of tragic mass shootings that pepper the history of Colorado and the homophobic rhetoric Colorado Springs has enacted over the decades. Club Q represents life lost, families and friends in mourning. The violence of one person's actions ripped away the lives of people who did not deserve to die. The targeting of my city's queer community is painful, and my rage is real and valid. I work in Denver and have lived in the Springs most of my life. Whenever I tell people where I live, the first response is "Are you okay?" This response mostly comes from the fear that a fat Black queer woman isn't the typical representation of the Springs. And it's true, the Springs doesn't always feel safe for my identities, and yet there is a duality. I experience deep joy alongside the pain. These two things can be true at once. In most of the news reports on the shooting, the focus was on the history of violence and hate in Colorado Springs. I never saw the perspective that queer joy and happiness also exist here. I didn't read that queer people have always lived in Colorado Springs and that they add to the beautiful fabric of our community. Since I didn't see it, I wrote it.

Queer Joy Blooms Here

Queer joy lives in Colorado Springs.
It has and always will take root and bloom.
Will cover the hate state legacy and biting evangelical speech, and propagate a rainbow garden.
Beautiful and vicious.
We are the petals and the thorns.
Leave us to grow our trans youth. Ensure they feel safe in their city, school, and home. Make sure they see themselves reflected in history and the future.
Flourish BIPOC queer identities. Intersectional understandings of how the sun impacts our growth in different ways.
Reinforce anti-racism in queer space is the only way to keep our soil nutrient-rich.
We are English ivy.

We'll wrap around our community.
Cover up the institutions supporting doctrines of hate.
Become family to those who don't speak to theirs anymore.
We will cheer for you at Pride.
Offer hugs and love at weddings.
Shop with you to find out how you want to greet the world.
Dance to songs where she is in love with her.
We will love.
We will be what we need.
Reflect that the queer community is thriving and climbing higher.
We do so with beat faces and durags.
Acrylic nails and binders.
In drag and in ballroom.
Hiking and exploring.
Laughing and singing.
We are a field of wildflowers, untamed and dynamic.
Queer joy is rage, is anger, is righteous indignation.
It is the poisons we produce to protect ourselves, our youth, and our legacy.
Cultivate the sweet sound of our names and our pronouns.

Our main harvest is queer elders.
Remind us that growing old is not an exception for queer lives.
Remind us that we do, and will, survive to embrace death in old age as a friend instead of an ambush.
Elders who didn't think they'd make it past twenty are teaching new generations how to grow.
Even when the weather is harsh, they show us it can be done.
We will lay bouquets into arms instead of on top of caskets.
Hang flags on city hall on a Tuesday just because.
Because no queer folks died today.
Because queer folks fell in love today.
Because queer folks lived today.
Queerness is not a funeral waiting to happen, it is life waiting to be lived.

And we are living.
We are thriving.
We are we are we are.
Queer joy will fortify the dance floors.
Sharpen high heels.
Lighten the loads we all carry.
Continue to share stories of those taken so we may never lose their lights.
Queer joy anoints the scars, binders, packers, and gender euphoria and names them holy.
Our garden is sacred, no longer secret, but a creation of our love.
Look closely and you'll know why queer joy blossoms here.

Grieve

Grieve, my people
Abandon all inhibition
Convulse and contort
This is your dance
Thrash about
Take up space
Fill it with your breath
Scream and wail
Baptize your body in tears
Fall, crumble, collapse
The earth will hold you
Call upon all who will listen
Cypher
Burn it down
Warm yourself near the flame
Find comfort in the life of the fire
Complete the emotion
See it all the way through
There is no end to grief
There is only integration
Grieve, my people

One of the strangest experiences of grief and mourning is the muscle memory. Our bodies remember and expect the same movements or actions even after someone is gone. After the death of my first dog, I continued to open the back door slowly, as if my dog would be sleeping by the door. Logically I knew he wasn't here anymore, but my body kept moving around him. These accidental movements have helped me recognize and release into my grief.

Muscle Memory

I didn't know I was grieving until I unclenched my jaw and dropped my shoulders.
I guess your death settled in between my molars and filled the space between my neck and shoulders.
My body attempted to save you.
Clenched to keep you close.
It's been a week, and I never noticed my body tightened at the news of your passing.
Until I unclenched my jaw, dropped my shoulders, and dealt with the grief I wasn't allowing myself to release.

After the death of George Floyd, I received texts from dozens of White people I hadn't talked to in decades, asking if I was okay. Some asked me to explain what was happening in society, and others apologized. I realized I must be the only Black person these people knew. I hadn't talked to some of them since second grade, and the murder of a Black man had inspired a check-in. I also saw some of these people posting about how they reached out and how they were being an ally. I personally don't love the word "ally" as an all-encompassing term to describe the support of movements outside of one's lived experiences. Think of it like this: if I robbed a bank, an ally would be on the sidewalk yelling, "Yes girl, rob that bank, you deserve all the money." An accomplice in this work would be my getaway driver who would have a stake in the game. If I go down, they are going down too. An accomplice is what I'm looking for, someone who is willing to walk alongside me even when it's hard. Performative allyship inspired this poem.

Ally (White Woman)

You find me laying on the ground.
Gunshot smoke rising from my body.
Sirens fleeing the scene of their crime.
Bleeding out.
Barely breathing.
I reach out to you to help.
You take a video.
Ask me what happened.
Ask me what you can do to be an ally in this moment.
Ask what I did to get shot.
Tell me I was asking for it.
Must have been breaking the law.
Ask me if it was Black-on-Black crime.
Demand I educate you on police brutality.
Instruct me to pull myself up by my bootstraps.
Ignoring they stripped me naked before they shot me.

Show me pictures of Beyoncé.

Ask me why can't I be like other Black women.

Tell me not every Black person is oppressed, in fact some are more privileged than White people.

Ask how you're supposed to explain this to your kids.

You ask me to use my last breath to tell you it's okay.

Want me to stop applying pressure to my bullet wounds so I can hold you with my bloody hands, stroke your hair, make you feel seen.

Because how else will you learn if not from me, if not from the oppressed.

Because your liberal arts college taught you experiential learning is essential.

You start to feel better.

You leave me to die in the street.

Find the nearest crowd.

Start to cry.

Pass my bloodstains off as your own.

Say how sad you feel about the injustices against Black people.

Never tell anyone where you left my body.

Swallow my name.

Hashtag my death.

You feel empowered.

You feel like an activist.

You call yourself an ally.

The rhetoric of domestic violence and rape culture starts early. Society reinforces violence as synonymous with love. I can remember dozens of times when a boy pulled my hair or pushed me down, and a teacher or adult told me it was because he liked me. Just like that, I was taught boys and men will hurt you when they like you. Rape culture can literally kill us.

Jessica

Jessica dies in the end.

. . . But for now she is 7.
She likes buttercup yellow and dinosaurs.
Today she comes home from school, different.
She is lightning storm and earthquake.
Mother asks about her day.
Her mouth can't hold the words and they mudslide like decaying earth.
"Um . . . During craft time I sit in the front with the blue chair and I was drawing unicorns, the sparkling kind,
and I named one princess,
and then my hair was on the floor?
Mommy,
The boy who sits behind me had scissors.
He laughed at me . . .
. . . I miss my hair."
Mother sighs,
relieved, like the words are negative test results.

"Oh, baby . . .
Boys are 'weird' like that sometimes.
Get used to it. It's normal.
Don't be scared.
Everything's okay.
Your hair will grow back."

Jessica is 13.
Full of questions and exploration.
She loves math and the taste of cinnamon.
Bobby's cute,
but he chases her at recess.
Pushes her onto the gravel.
This time,
Jessica stays down.
Cries monsoon for her bloody knees.
The teacher saw the attack and ran to her.
Jessica tries to shrug it off, says,
"Um . . . I fell.
Tripped over my feet.
I'm just clumsy.
That's why I'm a mathlete, not a track star . . ."
The teacher smiles knowingly.
Tells her,
"Bobby must have a crush."
Says,
"He must admire you.
Just got 'carried away' while
trying to push you out of his mind."
Says,
"Jessica, these are growing pains.
This is womanhood."

Jessica is 16.
Likes fanny packs and glasses.
Since they broke up Grant bullies her every day.

Calls her ugly.
Sends hateful notes.
Posts private photos.
She cries in the bathroom.
Cowers from the cafeteria during lunch.
Needs relief from her state of emergency.
Mother suggests she talk to a "professional."
Therapist asks why she's there.
She is articulate,
but slips back to mudslides.
Spills secrets of her body
being hashtagged and trending:
"#revengeporn #teenwhores"
How Grant's "pet name" for her is slut.
How he touched her
when she pretended to be asleep.

She leaves the session feeling better.
Goes to school the next day.
Gives Grant
   . . . another chance to make it work.
Learned,
she wasn't reading the signs right.
He still loves her.
Wants her back.
Even thought herself silly
for almost letting him go.

Jessica is 21.
She loves red roses and Beyoncé.
And Spencer.
They've dated for a while.
She knows it's love because
he tells her how to cut her hair.
And sometimes pushes her down.
Tells her she's not pretty enough

and how to be prettier just for him.
He touches her where he wants.
Whenever he wants.

He is the perfect guy.

Sometimes wipes off her makeup.
Calls her a slut, just like her first love.
Kicks her in the ribs until she earthquakes with pain.
Apologizes again for the volcano of his temper.
She keeps confusing lava burns for love.
Buttercup bruises cover her face and she can't smell cinnamon through her broken nose.
She still loves Beyoncé.
Listens to "Crazy in Love" on repeat.
She crumbles to earth . . . On repeat.
Is buried in dirt . . . Only once.
Wonders who will find her fossils and if they'd say hers was a true love story.

Bloom

People get mad when you grow.
They haven't spent time planting themselves.
Can't understand what it feels like to be resilient in harsh surroundings.
To be buried and nurtured by warmth and water.
To all of us sprouting and blooming, give these seeds something to talk about.
Unfold and stretch into who you are.

This poem saved my life. I was in a bad relationship in college, and as a result, I started writing more poetry. At the time, I thought I had hit an artistic groove, but in reality, I was working through my understanding of my relationship and my desire to get out. The bones of this poem started while I was in that relationship, and years later I was able to finish it. When you're in a bad or abusive relationship, it can feel like you've lost yourself and you're less powerful. I felt like I couldn't get out of his shadow, and no one could hear or see that I needed help.

No matter what situation or relationship we are in, we never truly lose ourselves or our strength. The sun does not become less powerful during an eclipse. Our power never leaves us. We are still dynamic, incredible beings, no matter our situations or relationships. This poem continues to help me remember my worth.

Big Bang Expansive

She is big bang expansive! Takes up universal presence. She is not colonized by man.
Emits meteorite laughter, cries constellations, and her smile, supernova combustion.
Over time she learns to be more planet than galaxy.
Knows her meteorites will burn up in the atmosphere of his presence.
Notices her body's boundary rings are not welcome in his space.
Starts to be sucked into his gravitational pull.
Told to revolve around someone's son.
Her sonic voice will never escape his black hole.
She is eclipsed.

Eclipsed by his shadow she becomes easy to forget.
But she is fireball nebula.
Her solar flares disrupt his darkness.
The speed of light can escape a black hole and she's never slowed down.

She dances northern lights and sings solar system hymns.
Fashioned an asteroid belt around her milky way and reclaimed
her space.
Her halo can be seen for light-years. Her body expands to
the outer limits.
She is more galaxy than planet. Her meteorite laughter is
fucking shit up.
She is big bang expansive.
She always has been.

Sex Appeal

I am the sexiest
When my mouth is wide open
And I speak my mind

Word Play

Don't put your words in my mouth.
Shove them down my throat.
Choke me on your punctuation.
Make me regurgitate expectations of how you think I should
be a woman.
Yes, your words are enormous and extensive and exaggerated.
They've been forced in many mouths.
But not this queen.
I prefer short sturdy words like consent, choice, and equity.
I won't be your oral fixation.
"No" feels better on my tongue than your outdated patriarchy.
I'd rather spit out your venomous masculinity than swallow
down your inadequacies.
You always think I want it.
Push my head down like I'm studying Hooked on Phonics.
Want me to go deeper.
Yell at me not to use teeth when I enunciate your words.
Don't want me to drag across your diction.
Because that feels a little too much like friction.
And I know you like your lexicon smooth and soft and
malleable.

Stop asking, "Why you so sad, girl?"
This mouth won't smile for you.
Trust me, my bitch isn't resting and this snarl is yours.

I've decidedly displayed disinterest.
My face doesn't take orders from entitled men on streets.
This is not an invitation for you to control me.
Patrol the way I react to your interaction.

Thank you, for saying I'd look more beautiful if I smiled.
You'd look more handsome if you shut up.
But men like you aren't good at taking directions.
Don't ask, "What that mouth do?"
I'm sure you can't handle the complexities, fantasies, and
daggers a flick of this tongue can manifest.
The way I effortlessly repeat rhythmic retro radio hits.
Suck my teeth in disgust.
Kiss you goodbye.
Blow bubbles, lick lips.
Bite back, clap back.
Redact your repulsive rhetoric.
Spit out what you've shoved down my throat.
Taste alphabets of my own substance
Fuck up your phrasing with a hard side-eye
Savor only songs of myself.

But the most important thing this mouth do is say **me too**.

And always louder than
"Boys will be boys."
"She asked for it."
"It's her fault."

Say "me too" when everyone is watching.
Say "me too" when no one is around.
Say "me too" when it stands for you, too.
For too many of us for a lifetime.

So keep your words in your mouth and learn how to swallow
your pride.

A Lesson in Rape

As girls, we are taught many lessons.
Cross your legs when you sit.
Pointing is rude.
Chew with your mouth closed.
And how not to be raped.

We are taught never go out alone, especially at night.
If caught, the streetlights will turn you into wounded prey for
the uncaged lions we are too afraid to tame.
They tell us groups of two or more are best.
There is power in numbers.
Taught to become Wolverine.
Weaponize our bodies
Place upright keys between tight knuckles.
Aim high.
They say we eat with our eyes, and he wants to consume the
pieces of your flesh he finds weakest, finds tastiest.
Blind him of this hunger
Being alone at night will get you raped.
So I learned to fear darkness.

When it does happen do not yell RAPE.
Don't be so obvious.
Yell FIRE instead.
Fire spreads and catches.
Has the potential to destroy and burn.

Produce ash out of skyscrapers.
As if my body is not building enough to burn.
That rape is not catching.
Not spreading through these hunting grounds we call streets,
and schools, and families.
Like the black asphalt isn't just a collection of women's burn
marks where she yelled fire instead of rape, and he engulfed
her flames.
So I learned to fear my voice.

We are taught drinking too much gets you raped.
You must be sober to defend against his advances.
Avoid jungle juice.
We women are susceptible to sweet things.
Never go upstairs at the party.
Don't leave your drink.
Take turns watching as you pee.
A left drink will get you drugged, get you raped.
Never take a drink from a stranger, he wants to rape you.
Watch the bartender make the drink.
Fix your gaze like he is a magician and you are his competition.
So I learned to fear my eyes.

We are taught, do not leave the house hungry.
Someone will feed you.
Translation, don't look like you want it.
Someone will rape you.
Your clothes have to be baggy.
Don't share the outline of the dinner you hold in your body.
Leave something to the imagination.
Make him work for it.
He can smell your bare skin.
Follow the scent like Pepé Le Pew.
Cover up your snacks and the breadcrumbs he follows to the
insides of you.
So I learned to fear my body.

I learned to fear myself.
But I learned to survive.
I practiced my lessons.
Learned from others who failed.
Saw every fourth girl in class become a teaching tool, become
next week's essay prompt.

I learned how to be a girl.
How to make it to woman.
Learned to cross my legs so no one can enter.
That pointing at injustice is too obvious.
How to close my mouth before someone fills it.
But the lesson I learned and questioned every day.
Is why our school was always in session, while the boys got
to play.

Chemical Reaction

Our love is chemical.
Like actual chemistry.
Like Bill Nye on some real shit.
Periodic elements and test tubes.
We are dynamic.
Me, all Coke-bottle body, sweet with brown-sugar skin.
You, fresh-to-death Mentos.
We, an unlikely pair.
The reaction of our interaction is only a fraction of our potential.
See, baby, when you're inside me, I can't help but explode,
such a sweet sticky mess, rising high to the sky.
This is what happens when we're together.
A chain reaction, a split-second contraction.
Leading to an eruption of me and you.
Ain't nobody makes me feel the way you do.
Pushing every button.
Causing me to wind up, to ramp up, to blow up.
Until I flip my top, hop on top so I can ride the wave of my
bubbling passion.
Until I am filled with our chemical reaction.

Catch & Release

The magic of sex is less about the physical intertwining of bodies and more about the release of shame and the freedom to experience pleasure.

To run after it.

Chase it with abandon.

Hold it momentarily, then release it to catch again.

Do As I Say

Tells me not to scream
As his tongue traces love spells
Between my wet lips

For Fat Women When Sex Feels Impossible

You are beautiful.
Your insecurities are not mountain enough to impede your pleasure.
Go to bed with him, with consent. The sexiest foreplay there is.

You've been wet since he kissed you. Fantasized about the ways his fingers would dance inside of you. Don't deny yourself his touch.

He knows what you look like. He knows you are fat and wants to fuck you too.

I know it's easy to think we don't deserve sex, that anyone could find our bodies erotic, but we are a collection of nerve endings waiting to be stroked. More woman to love. Tonight, love yourself and get what you want.

When you get home, take off your clothes. Striptease and teach him about your shape. Introduce him to the parts of you worth knowing—and every part is worth knowing. Leave nothing between you and him.

Your weight is not an elephant in the room, it is the sexiest thing in the room. You are meant to be seen, don't obstruct his view.

Each stretch mark is a treasure trail to your pussy. Ask him to start at the top and lick his way down. Encourage him to wade around in the river you've produced. Your thick thighs are pillows while he eats you.

Do not make yourself small. Stay large. Practice spreading yourself, opening up for pleasure. Swell and be filled with him. Relax your muscles and enjoy. The only thing tight on you is that pussy.

Keep the lights on. Let him discover your body like braille. You are gorgeous on your back.
As he enters his thrusts will wash through you like waves, each ripple tells a story of desire. Your stomach is sexy as fuck. Use your vibrations to stimulate his cock. Send earthquakes through your pussy and make him cum.

Get on top. Become the conductor of your orgasm. Ride him like he's the last horse out of town and you stole some shit. Don't stop until you climax. Your sweat is just proof you're almost there.

Never apologize for your weight. Bounce up and down. Hypnotize him with the way your body moves. Steady his hands on your hips. Let him grip your love handles. Use them to push himself deeper into you. Don't be afraid to break the bed. Put all of your weight into every thrust. Your brick-house body is built to last.

When your stomach touches his, smile. Don't hold your breath. Exhale onto him and keep going, we still have work to do.

Sit on his face, if he dies he dies, but he won't. He will not suffocate. He can handle your body.
Your weight does not matter in this room tonight. His face is your throne and you are his queen.

Angle yourself. Let his tongue explore your clit. You are Sacagawea, so you gotta help him navigate.

Support yourself on the wall. Brace yourself for when his licks become electric. You are beautiful in this pose. Take breaks. Listen to your body. Say no when you need to. Scream yes when you want. Breathe. Moan. Scream.

Give into yourself and over to him. Allow yourself to forget there was ever a reason to be afraid, to think sex wasn't built for a fat girl. Find positions that work for you.

Each time you scream "God," you are praising yourself. Arch your back, bite your lip, pull him closer and cum. Come to the realization we are sexy in every position.

Our weight does not determine how good the sex is, because baby it's always good.
Our partners can carry our bodies. Sex is collaboration, a balance, a sharing of spirit.

When it's done lie with him, no blankets, no sheets. You are a masterpiece of eroticism.
A naked muse.

Remember, we big women are not lucky to be fucked. They are lucky to fuck us.

Body neutrality has been an incredibly powerful place for me to land in my personal self-love journey. Body positivity, for me, wasn't always realistic. There are times when I don't want to or can't be positive about my body. There wasn't a large enough range of emotions within this movement. I noticed that when I felt the most beautiful, I wasn't actually thinking about my body, I was just existing. I would be dancing without focusing on how my body looked. I love the idea that bodies are just bodies doing body things. Coming to that conclusion gave me a new love and appreciation for all the things my body can do and helped me respect the limitations of my body.

Bodied

My body bodies in the most beautiful way that a body can body.

My body wants to body any other body that tells me what my body should be bodying.

My body bodies in a way that uplifts my body as the ultimate image.

My body bodies beautiful because it is my body.

Abundance

My cheeks are tight from smiling
My stomach is jiggling from laughing
My shoulders are down
My jaw is relaxed
My eyes are wide
My feet are firmly grounded
Joy is a full-body engagement

Break Up Poem

Finally ripped up the letter you gave me.
Thought better than to burn it, lest you phoenix from the ashes.
Turn forest to wildfire.
So I placed you with paper plates, old Chinese food, and things
I've already consumed.
Let your words rest quietly, they've already lied to me and I
want to remember you in pieces.
Fragmented promises and echoed I love yous.
you
you
You are trash can liberation.
A reminder you're unworthy of revisiting.
Letters aren't always meant to be cherished.
No shoebox with pictures and forgotten charms.
The emptying of you is endless.
Won't stop for mercy.
Constantly purging.
Leaving me with empty hands meant for receiving my own
scriptures.

Rape culture has been around for centuries, and no matter what time period you look at, the ideas have been the same. The blame and shame were pinned on a woman, based on her clothes or actions or whereabouts, instead of on the perpetrators.

Slut-Shaming

Boys be like . . .

Send that bitch a carriage.
Yeah, with a big horse and a velvet interior.
Shit, I heard she wears nothing under her petticoat.
Get this, the reason she's not married is because her and her suitor were caught in bed together.
They strung up the stained sheets for everyone to see.
What a whore.

Send that bitch an oil self-portrait.
Bitches love self-portraits.
I heard she will court anyone and her father doesn't even give away a dowry.
Get this, I heard at night, she shows her ankles behind the big apple tree.
What a slut.

Send that bitch a dick pic.

Bitches love dick pics.
Have you seen her on Tinder?
She's practically naked.
My friend knows her and she's slept with a bunch of dudes.
You're definitely going to get laid.
Just. Swipe. Right.

When did the clothes I choose to adorn this thick and curvy
body define my right to choose?
I said no, but my see-through shirt said yes?
My tight skirt said I wanted it?
And my lace underwear said I was asking for it?

I never thought my clothes would betray me in ways my
innocence will never forget.
My turtleneck choked the screams out of my mouth and turned
them into moans in his head.
The bare skin on my hands was just enough exposure to say
I did everything to turn on his self-righteous indignation to
thrust his weakness into something powerful.

That night my lipstick was just the right shade of red to cause
bulls and men to act with abandon.
My five-inch heels were bigger than his self-worth.
But that's just too much reality coming from my Jimmy Choos.

My fights and hits became electric sounds.
Switched to philharmonic.
Willed his violation turn into violins.
His wailing moans mimicked cellos.
His grunting bellowed like a throbbing bass.
His panting pounded like racing percussion.
Sounded like a cacophony of strings.
My head slams like tympani on the headboard.
Desperate fists thrashing with woodwind screams.
I became a symphony.

I composed my cries into a long chorus.
Bright blasting fury of hallelujah brass.
I turned symphony.
Do not confuse this sound with a masterpiece.
I was forced into music.
For survival.

He played me like an instrument, but they will say I was the
conductor.
Coerced him with my bedroom eyes.
Seduced him into sight-reading my body.
That I liked the sway of his song.

They will say shame, you slut.
They will say shame, you whore.
They will say shame, you bitch.

If we have to shame someone, shame the ones who are raping
us.
No metaphors.
No literary devices.
Shame the rapists.
Not our stolen bodies.

Alphabet Entitlement

Aggressive
Boys believe
Cat calling
Damsels
Equals
Free five finger
Grabs and gropes
Hoping
Indecent
Jokes
Keeps
Ladies
Mesmerized
Never
Owning their
Problematic patriarchal
Queasy
Rhetoric
Socialized
To think
Unwanted
Violations
Will
Xenomorph
Your
Zipper consent

Sharpened Smile

We do not owe you a smile.
Do not owe you any forced action.
The patriarchy will never be crowbar enough to open my lips.
Smiling does not make our femininity or our women-ness
valid.
Our frowns are crescent moon magnificent.
Straight lips are barbed wire between you and the barking
dogs we keep on our tongues.
Upturned lips in disgust are works of art, you are our muse.
We do not owe you our bodies.
But you sure as shit owe us an apology.

Battle Cry

It's okay to cry in battle.
May the outline of your strained tears serve as war paint
when you fight.

In 2020, the increased recognition of police violence and racism led to the mass circulation of police brutality videos depicting the deaths of Black people. People often shared the videos with no warning of violent and horrific murders. Society reinforced that such deaths were a common occurrence by how many thousands or millions of times the videos were shared without censorship. I can't remember the last time I saw a White person get killed or die in a viral video.

This poem is about the death of Ahmaud Arbery. He was a Black man who was murdered in a racially motivated crime while jogging. Someone sent me the video of his murder with no warning or context and it felt like a landmine. I died a little bit as I watched this man die In other cases, videos like this one appeared on timelines and "for you" pages, and they would explode with Black death on unsuspecting scrollers. Those same videos would have millions of views. Empty likes next to the murder of a Black man on repeat. Social media became the Black market to view Black death.

Landmine

You woke up
Saw Black death
Shared post
No warning
Just timeline landmine
I woke up
Thumb landed on Black death
Heard click
Forced to stay still
To read
To see
Dead Black body
White murder weapon
My hand shook
The mine exploded

More Black death
More likes for your post

The stereotype and the rhetoric that Black people don't do outdoorsy things dispossess us of the land that has always been a part of our culture and heritage. I have been working on reintegrating myself into nature, and organizations like Blackpackers that foster outdoor equity have helped me on this journey. As a part of Poetry719's weeklong poetry festival, we host a poetry and hiking event with Blackpackers. This piece came from a writing prompt on the trail. The difficulty of navigating it and learning about nature felt similar to my own discovery of myself: complex, difficult, and ongoing.

Uncharted

The descent inside myself is terrifying.
I'm unable to predict the trails.
The foliage appears to have turned against me.
I ask the trees to support me on this journey.
Lean on their rooted wisdom for this trek.
I'm not used to the geography of myself.
I've only seen maps drawn by topographers who colonized my land.
My native landscape has yet to be discovered.
There are canyons of sedimentary rock left from the erosion of my sentiments.
I do not know when I will return.

Sacred Touch

I challenge you to touch yourself.
Rub the parts you try to forget.
Grab fat.
Trace stretch marks.
Clap thighs.
Do not wait for someone else to explore your body.
You deserve to know how beautiful you feel.

There's a social media trend called a "body check." Someone will wear baggy clothes, typically a shirt, to appear bigger, and then they will pull the clothing tight to show the true outline of the body and reveal they were never fat. This trend reinforces that fatness or even appearing fat is bad, and the turn of the video is the surprise that reveals they are actually small and skinny. Body checks happen in a variety of ways, such as when asking someone their size, weight, or measurements and assigning value based on the answers. My weight fluctuates all the time, and I hold my weight in such a way that people are often surprised by my measurements. I was inspired by the anonymity of measurements and sizes as an act of defiance against body checks.

Body Check

I weigh a three-digit number. The order of which changes with my fullness.

My breasts are a combination of letters and numbers to fit the expansiveness of my back and chest.

Waist a home for beads that fall and rise as I do.

My hips measure wide in inches but are best captured as a pendulum when I walk.

I do not owe you numbers or letters to body-check me, instead check out this body being beautifully bodied by me.

Knees

I don't have Meg Thee Stallion knees
I have pop lock and drop it knees
Swag and surf knees
Drop it low knees
Do it for the 99 and the 2000 knees
Window to the wall knees
Krumping knees
Dancing on top of tables knees
Wack save the last dance knees
Icy Hot knees
I'm staying in tonight knees
My knees had their time knees

The prompt was "Write a love letter to a part of your body that could use some extra love." I have struggled with body image for most of my life. I always felt I wasn't skinny enough or wasn't curvy enough. I didn't see my body type growing up, and I struggled with self-love and honoring. I now am so in love with my body and all the ways it shows up; this poem was part of that journey to deep self-acceptance.

Dear Hips

Dear hips, you are one bad bitch.
The way you knock things off tables, it's like you were born to fight, born to be outlandish.

You sway like politicians' platforms and I am in awe of you.
Hourglass me and tick time in my womb.
You can seduce these wanting eyes, then push out our next generation of warriors.

Dear hips, you keep my fanny pack up, you keep my spirits up, and I've got mad respect for your symmetry, the way you divide my femininity in two.

As J. Cole says, "One time for my LA sisters, one time for my LA hoes."
But my hips make me both.
I'm the natural sister with stretch marks, kinky curls, cocoa butter, and no filter.
And I'm the hoe rocking a blonde wig, fake nails, a push-up bra, and someone else's eyelashes.

I am duality.
You are duality.
You allow me to transition, chrysalis, and kaleidoscope.

I don't show you enough love. I try to push you hoping to
restrain you, but you pop back like Pop Rocks and pop off
like the street cats that catcall these big bones, and all y'all
show love to these thick thighs.

It's time I start praying to the whole body. Giving honor and
reverence to my ladies, to these hips.

Fit In

I bought a dress I couldn't fit in.
Tried it on and fell in love with the way it made my body sing.
The zipper was a wide canyon on the landscape of my back.
No amount of deep inhales or Spanx could close this gap.
I never felt more beautiful.
Standing in a full-length mirror in the dressing room at Ross.
Gazing at the girl I'd risk it all for.
My smile finally reached my eyes and I swear I stared for hours.
Felt like I'd met the woman I've been trying to become.
In a junior's formal gown, I fell in love with myself as I am,
with no desire to change or fit in.
Happy to finally see myself clearly.

Play Date

Become best friends with every inch of your body.
Honor the pinky toes.
Praise the kneecaps.
Run fingers over scars and remember survival.
You deserve to know your own love.

I love piercings for aesthetic enhancement, but what I love even more is how attentive you become to your body. There is a sense of curiosity as we heal, and intentionality behind our self-care. Piercings are all about healing and adjusting to new landscapes. This is one of my favorite poems and a reminder of how to take care of my body.

Attention

There is beauty in the healing process.
The dutiful care of the body after a trauma.
Prepare the ritual.
Mixed elixir of salt and warm water as purification.
Cotton swabs wrapped in ancestral prayers for cleansing.
The sting and burn and throbbing are reminders that pain means healing, and pain can lead to beauty.

After this trauma I am more careful with my body.
Protective of threats.
Cautious of my surroundings.
I am present in my body.
Know her needs and wants.
Satisfy them as they present.

Notice the way skin makes room for the holes.
How the body rebuilds when a piece of you is taken.
Praise the fading memory of pain.
The ability to forget the trauma.
Choose the aesthetic to signify a battle won, to signify survival.

The Breast Speaks

We are tired of being covered up.
Called explicit and inappropriate.
Sexualized and fetishized.
Realize that we we have fed nations.
Raised queens, kings, leaders, and warriors.
Know all too well, the act of giving of ourselves to others.
Swell to provide for you.
Call us brujas.
Forgotten elders.
Mixing potions and elixirs for our kin.
We are in abundance
We are a spectrum.
Some of us are large and round.
Praise us for the way we can hold bountiful life and comfort.
Others are long and narrow.
Honor us for continuing our ancestral legacy.
Stretched from mouths, stretched from growth.
There are those who are small and pointed.
Celebrate us for being everything that's needed.
There is beauty in the pigment.
Creamy dark skin, chestnut caramel stretch marks, and warm
chocolate areolas.
Each of us is a reflection of womanhood, a legacy, a connec-
tion to our power.
Let us stand in silence.

In reverence.

In love.

For those of us who have not made it.

Who offered themselves up.

Cut away leaving survival scars tended to with sacred oils and prayer.

So we ask, touch yourself.

Touch us.

Give us focused attention.

Know that we feel as much as you do.

Learn more about us, and by doing so learn about you, about our legacy.

We are more than just skin and fat.

We are more than societal markers of sexy.

No longer confined to wire supports.

Strapped down and forced up.

We are full frontal.

And we are free.

Reflection

Your body is banging.
Your aura is glowing.
I can see your chakras align from a mile away.
Your mind is expanding.
Your soul is healing.
I love to see you this way.

Morning Ritual

I felt beautiful today.
Fresh from the shower, I checked myself out in the mirror
and thought,
Damn!
I'm hot.
I'm a babe.
I've got ass for days.
I'm a bad bitch.
Yass queen!
Get it!

Then, I wiped away the steam on the mirror and it really hit me.

I am sexy!
I'm a baddie.
I can pull guys off eye contact.
I am a goddess.
Attractive as fuck.

It's important you know I haven't lost any weight.
I, a French bakery, each roll delicately and intentionally placed
on display.
My stretch marks, a roadmap to a private island of wildflowers.
The bulge in my stomach reminds me there is room to grow.
Thick thighs a symbol that more of me is a gift from God.

Reminds me friction is not always bad.
How to let things fall and trust they will be caught.
Arms that jiggle tell the world there is rhythm in every part
of my body.
Shows how close to flying I can come while standing still.

There are these moments after hot showers when I stand in
awe of a body I have the privilege of inhabiting.

Welcome Home

My brick-house body is the kind wolves have trouble destroying.
I am fortified with concrete trauma.
Poured in by masons who promised it would make me stronger.
Each brick a shade of red for the blood my ancestors left in
the soil as they hung.
Strange fruit foundation.
I touch my frame to feel close to my past.

I got a big fat attic where I hide my skeletons.
Sometimes I swear they play hide and seek.
Show up unannounced.
In closets.
At dinner parties.
They mean no harm.
Just miss what it feels like to be noticed.

My kitchen is blessed with sage and grease.
There are worn cookbooks and almost-empty spice racks.
My kitchen is large like my ability to nurture.
My garden windowsill is magic, is earth and root and water
I practice giving birth, growing and mourning life in each pot.

The furniture is old.
Smells like incense and fried chicken.

The cushions are deflated from long conversations over wine
and card games.
The bedrooms are always talking.
The wallpaper whispers affirmations.
My carpet sings inspiration each time I enter.

I am a home all to myself.

Rendezvous

Melanin and the sunrise are old friends.
They often meet in the early morning at the intersection of
my beauty and radiance.
I welcome them with open arms and a smile.

Black Lives Matter

Black people have been hunted for so long it can be easy to forget the battles we are fighting within our minds. Our mental health matters.

Serpentine

Healing is not Lnear.
There is beauty in the waxing and waning of our hearts.
We are gorgeous in the process.
We are powerful in the pain.

Depression is something most people understand, but it is so difficult to explain. Even as a therapist, it's hard to find the words to embody what depression feels like. I chose to use personification for this piece to show how the complexity of depression is similar to a bad relationship or a fuckboy you can't quit. I was inspired by the "depression kitty" from the show Big Mouth. I thought it was an incredible way to describe depression and wanted a similar vibe for this piece. I also want to portray that going for a run won't fix my depression; just smiling through it won't change it. I want to show it is a real, pervasive experience.

Fuckboy

Depression is a fuckboy.
He texts me at 2 a.m. and asks if I'm still up.
Ravages my body until I am left bare and he escapes under the cracks of my door.
He just wants to be friends even after I have replaced everyone else with him.
I know he is with other people.
I can tell just by looking at them.
There is an empty longing in the eyes of those who have slept with him.
He makes cold our homes so he is the only thing to keep us warm.
I know he isn't good for me.
Fuckboys only want one thing, but it's different when I'm with him.
At least I can feel when I'm with him.
He's allergic to my smile.
Tells me I'm more beautiful with no expression.
Regularly takes my voice hostage.

Gets off on my silence.
Leaves me with cracked lips and a rough tongue.

Sometimes he makes me an offer.
Suggests we should have a threesome with his best friend.
I think about this often.
Anything to get his attention off me.
But his best friend Death doesn't seem like someone who
could stay in his lane.
I know if it happens at least I'll finally get away.
Maybe his best friend will be a better man for me.
Be the last relationship I'll ever have.
I linger on these fantasies.
Imagine what it would be like to have two things consume
me at once.
Who would take me first?
Which, the better lover?
But I keep coming back to depression, telling him I don't
want to share.
I can't risk losing the only person who understands me.

Our history is complicated.
We are childhood sweethearts.
I fell for him instantly.
His body made out of old bedsheets.
Pillow indentation hair.
Eyes an existential crisis.
I lose time when I'm with him.
Hours, sometimes days.
Can't remember my own name.
Forget I used to have a fiancé named Joy.
There are moments when I think I can leave him.
He is a weighted blanket and I am not strong enough to leave
his safety.
He always seems to know my next move.
How to keep me in my place.

He subtly mentions my insecurities.
How no one would want me.
He's the only one who knows how to handle hopelessness.
So I stop trying to leave him.
Succumb to his python embrace.
Realize we were made for each other.
I don't know who I am without him in my life.
Like who else could see beauty in my darkness?
Who else will spend hours in bed with me?
Who else will cut away pieces of me for his collection?
At least someone wants to put me on display.

I'm not ready to end it.
Not sure I ever will be.
Relationships aren't that simple.
I'm told to just leave.
Just be happy.
Just stop letting him control you.
I know he isn't good for me.
I know the way he makes me feel isn't normal.
But, I secretly wait for those 2 a.m. texts.
For his crippling touch.
With him, I'm not alone.

All I'm able to do is write this poem.
Hope someone who reads this shares the same fuckboy and
knows they're not the only one catching feelings for someone
who will never love them back.

Homeostasis

The absence of anxiety is like stillness after centuries of vibrations.

Fellow Travelers is a phrase Irvin D. Yalom used to describe a therapist and patient relationship. Rather than the therapist being the guide or leader, this phrasing suggests that the therapeutic experience is a journey both parties take, walking alongside each other in shared work. I wanted to create similar imagery in this poem to describe my experiences working as a therapist on an adolescent psychiatric unit.

Fellow Travelers

I am a holder of treasured stories.
Look for patterns in disorganized whispers.
Find maps to buried trauma.
Learn braille to know the language of cutting.
Read the raised scars like novels.
I am curious in the cycles.
Work hard to flow mania into art.
Create stillness from hyperactivity.
I am a weighted blanket to your anxiety.
I am a cushion to self-soothing.
We sit under tables and hide from our thoughts.
Play music to drown the voices.
I will cry with you.
Model that your pain is valid.
I am a friend.
Shake hands with minds who won't remember me.
Notice your delusions and replace them with poetry.
Use psychosis as a muse and provide the canvas.
Return you to the present.

Pull you out of formed realities.
Ground you in sensory exploration.
We learn and grow together.
I am tabula rasa for your projection.
Take misconceptions from your narrative so I can hold them
and lighten your load.
I am keeper of wonders.
I am on a journey with you.

Synergy

When melanin mixes with joy, it creates magic.

My name is "résumé proof"—meaning Ashley Cornelius has no cultural identifiers, which increases my ability to get a job. I often get surprised looks when my Black beautiful self shows up for an interview. More than a few times in my life, I've been told, "You weren't who I was expecting when I saw the name Ashley." One of my bosses once said it was a shame my name is Ashley because people won't know I'm Black when looking at the board list to prove there is diversity on the board. I've felt the harm of having a "White" name and have seen the harm to folks with less "White" sounding names. All of this is in quotes because it is a paradigm of language that isn't real but has real-world consequences. This poem was inspired by a conversation that came up a few years ago about certain employers saying they would never hire someone named Keisha, and the perpetual mockery of "Black" names. I thought about it and had the idea that Black people's names are a reclaiming of identity in the face of a diaspora that ripped away their names, heritage, culture, and language.

Names

We all have names we won't name our kids.
Basic names become hosting grounds for traumatic memories.

Brittany bullied me in middle school. Every insult internalized
my oppression, convincing me that I would never be enough.

Brian did nothing wrong, he just had a perpetual Oreo cookie
crumb around his mouth and it haunts me in my dreams.

Grant found blemishes on my body and used them as grenades
against my self-love. Called me ugly for every pimple, mole,
and scar he could see.

Michael, Brandon, Josh, Ethan, and Tyler all broke my heart.

Catherine taught me toxicity doesn't only belong to romantic
partners and can show up in all relationships.

Why risk naming my future child after people who have caused me pain?

Why risk naming my future child after people who have caused my ancestors pain?

John could have been the slave owner of my ancestors. Could have been the reason a whip cracking still scares me. Could have worked stolen souls to the bone and then snorted their dust to get high. Even in death, John used us to feel better about himself.

Lauren might have been the name of the wife who closed the door on the nightly rape of Black innocence. Listened to another woman pleading for help while she washed clothes, thinking, "Better her than me." Called the survivor a slut for letting herself be used by her husband.

Robert is a likely name of a top auctioneer who wore a smile like a medal as he sold mother, father, and son to diaspora and generational trauma. Took pride in the separation of Black families.

Elizabeth, the name of the master's baby raised on breast milk meant for the children my great-great-great-grandmother was never allowed to have.

We've all met the people we won't name our kids after, but Black people have to wade through the seas of names that could have, might have, a high probability of being the same name as our ancestors' rapists, capturers, and murderers.

Our last names are the branding of the families we belonged to. But at least we have control of our children's first names

We don't talk enough about forced assimilation.

Hearing employers say, "I would never hire a Keisha."
Knowing how easily Ashley gets a second interview.

We have to pick between résumé-proofing children's futures
and reinforcing a colorial legacy.
So we twist words and letters like Bantu knots and name our
children DeAndre, Ashuad, Tykeisha, Ebony, and Shavanda.

This is one way we know our babies will not carry the weight
of an oppressor's tongue on their name.
Even when we name our children Emily we spell that shit
Emmalee,—we will continue to disrupt the European stan-
dards of language.

We are making our own dialects.
We are starting with our children.
Taking back the pieces of our heritage still stuck to the whips
and chains displayed in museums.

We will teach our children that society will learn to say our
names.
The same way Dostoevsky feels comfortable in our mouths,
Jaykwon will leave a seasoned taste on our tongues.
Moeisha tickles the roof of your mouth.
Latasha goes down smooth like a fine scotch.
They are gonna say our names, as reparations for decades of
no names on unmarked graves.
They are gonna say our names.

Toy Guns

Black people cosplay
Have to decide if fake guns
Will cause their real death

Two Americas

He had a bad day, they said.
It's not his fault, they said.
Violent video games are to blame, they said.
He was bullied, they said.
A woman turned down his advances, they said.
He is a patriot, they said.
He has a gun license, they said.
He is a victim of the system, they said.
He deserves to live, they said.
He needs help, they said.
He's just a kid, they said.
He isn't a threat, they said.
He's hungry, they said.
He needs a bulletproof vest, they said.
We have to protect him, they said.
He didn't mean it, they said.
It's okay, they said.
It's okay he killed them, they said.

She was a threat in her sleep, they said.
She killed herself in her cell, they said.
He's a kid, they said.
He's an adult, they said.
He was resisting arrest, they said.
She was protesting her rights, they said.

It looked like a gun, they said.
He was a criminal, they said.
He was suspicious, they said.
She was running, they said.
He was walking, they said.
They were driving, they said.
He was existing, they said.
They got what they deserved, they said.
They were a threat, they said.
They don't need help, they said.
It was okay we killed them, they said.

One of the biggest shifts in my understanding of the world was realizing the system isn't broken. The conversations around systemic oppression often embrace the idea that the system isn't working well, that something went wrong, or that it has broken down over time. The reality of the situation is that the system is working perfectly. In fact, the more folks are oppressed, the more fine-tuned the system becomes. The system is a hell of a project. I mean, it has been doing the work of harming and keeping "order" for centuries. All of the hurt, harm, racism, homophobia, and injustice are direct products of the system. As Audre Lorde once said, "The master's tools will never dismantle the master's house." We have to break the system. This poem is my first swing at it.

The System Isn't Broken

The system is broken.
The corruption of the "system" is deep and historical.
It is our job as activists to fix, repair, and realign the system.
The justice system. School system. Prison system, Healthcare system. Economic system.

The system is not broken.
It's not that the innocent are falling through cracks and condemned to darkness.
Or that justice and equality have been eroded.
The system is working perfectly.
It is protecting and serving the great-great-great-grandchildren of founding fathers.
It is oppressing and suppressing voices written as inferior in our Constitution.
In fact, by the time you finish this poem a rapist has picked up twenty pieces of trash as their punishment.
By the end of this sentence, the ink will have dried on a wrongful conviction of an innocent Black man.

The system never liked Black people.
Couldn't find ways to openly hunt us so they wove it into the fabric of our systems.
Made it legal to gun down innocent Black men.
Created laws to protect the killers.
Gave killers badges to protect the laws.

The system was designed so that Cyntoia Brown was sentenced and served fifteen years for killing a grown man who hired her, a young child, for sex.

Our system knows that men whose names don't get to be a part of this poem can rape a woman, unconscious, behind a dumpster and get off.

The system was constructed so Black and Brown bodies selling marijuana are imprisoned for most of their life, while White budtenders and dispensary owners gentrify and profit in their absence.

The system created the panic defense. Making a case in court that a person's sexual orientation, gender identity, or expression grants permission for someone to beat, torture, or kill them.

Our system is well oiled when there are more prison cells than schools.
When neighborhoods for Black folks are designed to block resources.
The fact there is a sixteen-year life expectancy gap for the southeast of Colorado Springs and the north of the city means the system is working.

If you are shocked by these atrocities, then you are forgetting the definition.
A system is a set of things working together as parts of a mechanism or an interconnecting network. An organized

scheme or method to support a driving force.

We were never supposed to learn how to drive.

The system couldn't fathom Black people would be in political power.

Never anticipated there'd be trans CEOs.

Didn't plan for women to become doctors and surgeons.

We are their worst nightmare.

We are the children of the brujas, the enslaved, the immigrants, the untouchables they couldn't kill.

We are surpassing and fucking up their expectations of perceived limits.

Our job is to break the system, to deconstruct foundations of oppressive cogs and wheels designed to harm us.

This poem is a sledgehammer.

Your engagement is a wrecking ball.

Our presence is a demolition of this system.

Where Have All the Black Men Gone?

There's a tale they leave for cigarettes and a carton of milk.
Step into unsuspecting portals in gas stations and refrigerated doors to be lost and unheard of again.
I know they are liquefied by police sirens and handcuffs on their way to the store.
Their viscous spirits erode badges to reveal Runaway Slave Patrol.
Spilled milk and loose cigarettes chalk outline where injustice strikes.
Gathered them up and poured them into jail cells like thick molasses until the system is Black and sticky and slow.
Leaving us to ask where have all the Black men gone?

Independence for Whom?

The Fourth of July
America's freedom day
We watched fireworks chained

Stockholm

A fifteen-year-old girl is heading home from school. She is a local, and knows the land the same way a fish understands water. She was raised by the community. She is the community. She is excelling in school and plays the violin. Her family is excited about what her future holds. It is broad daylight.

She is kidnapped.
Picked from the streets before she reaches home.
She is blindfolded and drugged.
The White men who take her are dangerous.
They tell her she is their property.
They take her ID and hold it for ransom.
They tell her, "Your name is Sarah now," after one of the men's mothers, a good Christian woman, unlike her.
They call her savage.
Spit at her feet.
Funny, how men treat women with disrespect in the name of God.
As if God is not a woman, is not a dark-skinned Black woman.
As if there will not be a reckoning against those who murder in her name.

They cut her hair.
Make her wear ill-fitting clothes as a reminder she is not deserving of comfort.

They rape her.
They beat her.
They use her.
She is their property.

This lasts for weeks.
For months.
For years.
She has a daughter by one of the White men.
There are moments when she forgets where she came from.
She says her name fondly.
Proudly shows off her ill-fitting clothes as precious gifts.
Strokes the bruises to feel close to the kidnappers.
She continues to cut her hair.
She believes she looks better this way.
She is allowed to leave the house.
She is called wife.
She wears a ring to signify who she belongs to.
She talks fondly of her husband. Says he saved her.
She tells her daughter her father is a good man, and that she
was conceived with consent.
She prays her daughter will marry someone like her father.
Other men are envious of how strongly she loves her husband.
How fiercely loyal she is to her family.

She lives the rest of her life pledging allegiance to her captors
daily.

She dies as a woman named Sarah.
She dies as the wife of her captor.
She dies a stolen girl.
She dies a missing person.
She dies enslaved.

Black people have forgotten we were stolen. Forgotten we
were raised by the community, that we are the community.

We were taken in broad daylight by White men who are
dangerous.

May we remember. Learn our names. Grow out our hair.
Take back our bodies.
And teach our children, these White men are dangerous.

I have had irregular periods most of my life. I would get on a plane, period. I would go on a hike, period. I would be in a different state, period. Birth control helped regulate my periods, but it took a long time and a lot of explaining to get to that solution. I imagine my period as a woman who wants to be believed, respected, and supported. She is bold and brassy and tired of the bullshit.

My Period

My period is a rogue witch.

She doesn't give a fuck about the moon and her cycles. She bleeds when she wants, for as long as she wants.

My period smudges with weed and makes protection circles with the ground bones of racist men.

My period has been known to stab a bitch . . . and by bitch, I mean me. She twists the knife so I know she's in control.

She calls herself an artist. Her medium finger paints. She uses my insides and favorite panties as her canvas.

Her idea of a good time is Hennessey and trap music. Makes beats with the sounds of White women crying at the consequences of their own actions.

Twerks to the continuous beat of women breaking the glass ceiling.

My period doesn't like change unless it's caused by her.

She invented CP time. She comes unexpectedly and expects to be greeted warmly.

She says, "Fuck the patriarchy."

Says she is the matriarchy.

My period is sensitive and shit. She loves romance novels and the smell of lavender.

My period is insecure. She is tired of being called "disgusting and nasty." She is broke from being taxed in order to maintain her health.

She is angry at the audacity. At the misinformation. At the toxic shock syndrome.
At the rough cotton, as if we haven't picked enough cotton for a lifetime.

My period has a lighter in one hand and a Molotov cocktail in the other, and says, "Try me."

My period deserves some goddamn respect.

Virginity is an incredibly interesting concept. Growing up in the church, I learned that a person's, and more specifically a woman's, virginity is her everything. It was a symbol of purity, grace, and desirability. Without it, you are a slut. Without it, you are used up. Without it, no one would want to marry you. Then, when you have sex, the language around it is violent and harsh—"bang, hit, smash"—and the focus is on the man "taking" a woman's virginity, giving the power to the sexual partner (typically a man) instead of the woman engaging in sex and pleasure. This poem is the reclaiming of my sexuality, power, and virginity.

Virginity

I lost MY virginity.
Misplaced it.
Couldn't find it at the bottom of the canyon of my sexuality.
Was told only my boyfriend could find it.
He was the only qualified person to navigate MY uncharted
territory.
Spelunker to this dark cave.

Some will say I was deflowered.
Had my cherry popped.
Others might call it becoming a woman.
Say he took it.
Stole it.
Settled MY body in his name.
Kept the title on his wall.
Trophied MY virginity and named it toxic masculinity enhancer.

I was told to give it up.
Said he'd waited long enough.
I owed him.
He earned it.
Because flowers, drinks, and dinner are an equal transaction for MY body.
He told his friends he smashed, banged, hit it, beat the pussy up like fight night.
Reinforced the way we make sex feel like violence.
Turned my body object.
Setting it in motion for years and years.
Knowing an object will stay in motion until acted upon by another force.
I am that force.

I stopped my body from spiraling.
I found MY virginity.
Rejected the idea MY body was supposed to be colonized by a man.
I became cartographer.
Mapped out the wild underbrush.
Charted the locations of MY precious resources.
Protected MY nation and declared myself queen.
Took control of when I let in foreign bodies.
Decided how long they can stay.
Won't let them roam without permission.
I will never give up this land.
Made an oath of protection never to lose MY virginity, but to give her willingly to each explorer I want to share in MY majesty.
I call this liberation.
I call this body mine.

The number of men who decided to get loud with me over the song "WAP" was extraordinary. This song came out during a period of huge social unrest and alongside the recognition that Dr. Seuss was racist. There were so many social media posts expressing sadness that Dr. Seuss's books were being "canceled" and songs like "WAP" were being produced. Of course, the children were brought into it, with comments about kids no longer having Dr. Seuss and listening to "WAP" instead. All of the rhetoric just reinforced that Black women's sexuality and pleasure are so powerful and beautiful that people feel threatened by the very thought of it. What I love about "WAP" is that it is purely talking about pleasure. The song only focuses on the needs of the women singing. There were protests against this song, news articles and videos about how inappropriate "WAP" was, while hundreds of other songs (largely by men) that reinforce rape culture, sexism, violence, and more, are considered classics. This poem is one response to the multiple conversations I had around this song. Thank you Cardi B and Megan Thee Stallion for this song.

WAP

To the man who said, "In times like these, how is 'WAP' the song they choose to put out?"
Implying during unrest and fear, wet-ass pussies are an ignorant response.

When we experience loss and death, we often turn to creation.
Wet-ass pussies are the perfect response.

May we honor the stillness with flowing and cleansing of warm wet floods.
Let me baptize this earth between my legs.
Let them drink from my fountain of pleasure.
When you feel rage, take a sound bath in my moans of euphoria.
When you ask for justice, bring me the guilty.

I will drown them, waterboard them, suffocate them with my thighs.
This pussy is for pleasure and destruction.
May I birth generations of activists, judges, and protestors.
May I birth the children who will burn down this system.
I will honor myself and our movement.
With pleasure.
With licks.
With strokes.
With vibrations.
Now is the time for WAP.
It is the perfect time to be wet.
To be warm.
To be reminded of creation.
To name pleasure a revolutionary act of resistance.

Yearning for Moonlight

The moon is the baddest bitch I know.
Stunts on us from her vantage point.
Bends our necks and gently tilts our chins so we may gaze
upon her iridescence.
Sometimes full frontal and all natural.
Sometimes drapes her black silk robe to reveal a sliver of her
shoulder.
I am always left wanting more.

I love the conceptualization of Mother Nature as a Black woman. This was a prompt I gave myself for Earth Day. I have always imagined Mother Nature as a beautiful, big, dynamic woman. The oppression of Black women is not unlike the way we treat the earth, and this comparison allowed me to focus on support of the earth and Black women.

Mother Nature

Mother Nature is a Black woman who is tired.

If the way you treat Black women is any indication of how we treat this earth, I am terrified.
She, a bruised and battered woman of generational trauma. She calls herself a survivor. Prides herself on being resilient. How she still grows after years of abuse.

You say she was asking for it.
"Showing off those precious resources like that."
"What were we supposed to do with a forest so thick like that? We drilled her and took what was ours. She didn't seem to mind."

You cut down her foliage in the name of progress. Put up houses and call this society. Tear down homes of living creatures and call this necessary.

Exploit her beauty. Sexualize her natural landscapes. Sell her by the square inch to the highest bidder. But isn't that how you treat most women?

Gaslight us. Make us feel crazy. Say we are making things up. Causing Mother Nature to get angry, to warm up, to square up. You call her hot flashes a woman's trouble. Can't you see that we're in trouble when she heats up and burns us down?

The ice caps are dripping, but all you hear is rap lyrics. She is burning up from your ignorance, but you call this fake news when all she asks for is the truth, is the recognition, is for us to come with the same energy to save her as we do to save ourselves.

The tornadoes are her pleading. The tsunamis are her cries. The earthquakes are her pounding on her chest. The storms are her yelling for us to listen.

Honestly, some of y'all never grew up with a Black woman and it shows. Never learned how to honor a Black woman. How to listen to her intently. How to protect her resources. Aid in the growth of her kingdom. Rebuild the parts of her she has sacrificed for her family.

This is how you treat a Black woman. How you treat Mother Nature. Gaia. Mother goddess.

She has been providing for us since the beginning of time. Benevolent offerings. Exponential love and care.

Her skin, dark and rich as the soil that brings forth life. Hair, coarse and curly foliage, a collection of ecosystems. The thick underbrush of her afro is shelter and warmth.

Her body, as in nature, does not have straight lines. She is overflowing with curves and bends. Her hips wide, full of oceans and waves. See how she is swelling and ebbing with every moment.

Her eyes are constellations. Guiding us home every single night. Her beauty is our responsibility.

We must protect Black women.
We must protect Mother Nature.

We must listen and believe when she tells us she is hurting, she is tired, she is worn.

We owe her reparations.
We owe her our survival.
We owe her to listen.

Etymology

Lunatic.
From the Latin luna. Derived from the belief that changes
to the moon cause insanity.
My menstruation is the cause of insanity.

Hysterical.
From the Greek hysterikos. Meaning suffering in the womb.
My body is the cause of suffering.

Friday the 13th.
An unlucky number, a cursed day.
13 cycles of the moon.
13 menstrual cycles.

We have been taught to fear the divinity of the feminine.
Code it as mental illness.
Name it unstable and scary.
Moons, wombs, blood, and magic.
Men have always feared that which they cannot control.

Black Moms

Black mothers are not your little friends. They ain't your friend Johnny's mom down the street. They don't really like the way his mom parents anyways.

Black mothers brought you into this world and can take you back out.

Black mothers don't know who the fuck you talking to like that. Don't remember raising their child to act like that.

Black mothers want to know who you think you are.

If you ask for McDonald's, they wanna know if you got McDonalds money.

When we get to the store, Black mothers tell us, "don't ask for nothing, don't touch nothing."

Black mothers teach us not to be around when grown folks is talking. Then talk about us to their grown folks friends loud enough for us to hear it.

Black mothers will slap the black off you. Might slap you into next week.

They ain't Boo Boo the Fool. Not certain anyone even knows who that is, but they ain't it.

Will tell you to stop crying before they give you something to cry about.

Black mothers call you tender-headed when they comb your hair. Tell you to hold your ear when that hot comb is near.

Ask if you live in a barn.

Whisper-scream through their teeth at church to "fix your face before I fix it for you," all while singing a hymn.

Black mothers tell you to keep playing and see what happens.

"Didn't I tell you" is Black mothers' way of saying "per my last email."

They tell us we smell like outside and to sit down somewhere.

Black mothers ain't playing with chu.

Tell us to get out of their sight.

Black mothers pay the light bills and we bet not be leaving lights on. Black mothers also pay the heat bill and we bet not keep the door open and let the heat out.

Black mothers thank God for everything, most importantly for their children.

Black mothers protect their kin. Will check anyone who messes with us.

Black mothers will fight for us and with us.

Black mothers don't play when it comes to their children.

Black mothers comfort us like no one else can.

Black mothers teach us how to survive. How to wake up under the weight of the world and handle our business.

They teach us they won't always be there, and how to keep going.

Black mothers make us strong.

Black mothers.

My mother.

Taught me how to be a Black woman.

Black women are not spirit animals. I've been told many times by White men and women that they have an inner Black woman or there is a Black woman trapped inside them or Black women are their spirit animals. Spirit animals have been commodified by White culture and are used in a problematic fashion, often disregarding the deep cultural significance to native and indigenous people. Then there is the added layer of White people wanting to act "Black"—snapping fingers, rolling their necks, and laughing about how they are really Black inside. I grew up hearing things like this over and over again. This is my response to years of people thinking my identity is a thing they can tap into when they're feeling sassy.

Spirit Animal

Black women are not spirit animals.
I am not your spirit animal.
We are not spirits, though you treat us like ghosts in this world.
Murder us, then wonder why you're haunted.
Why the wind sounds like moans between the trees you hung us on.
We are not animals, though you are in the business of caging and killing us for sport.

There is not a Black woman trapped inside of you.
You are not a magician, pretending Black girl magic is as easy as pulling our generational trauma out of a hat.
Watching Black men die in movies is not the same as watching our Black sons get slaughtered in the backyard.
Your White tears will never amount to the oceans our ancestors died in, decided to suicide in.
Chose to escape being assistant to sawing their families in half.
You can't fool us with sleight of hand and make our history disappear.

You love to say Black women are spirit animals, and aren't animals synonymous with savage and uncivilized?
Animals aren't treated well in your care
You might attempt to skin and wear my pelt because you wanna feel "down," wanna feel "woke."

You don't know what it means to be a Black woman and fight through adversity.
Survive for the babies born into a world actively trying to kill them.
How we teach children Skittles, Arizona tea, and toy guns are too much like weapons to hold.
Being sexualized for a big butt and wide hips, never forgetting the freak shows they put us in.
How much they paid to see these features behind bars.
How much we were sold for to the highest bidders.

Being a Black woman means my hips have carried generations.
My back is strong against your ignorance.
It means we are powerful.
Fighting every day to walk through a world made difficult for us.
Working twice as hard to get half of what they have.

We Black women are resilient.
Smell like shea butter and coconut oil.
Can push through systems built to destroy us.
Transform our hair with fingers and grease.
We Black women, make change.
March for change until our feet bleed.
Bend knees in prayer and protests.
Take up space.
Refuse to be your spirit animals so you can try to relate to the spirits that haunt you when the wind blows.

She Is Black

Sarah Rector became the youngest African American millionaire at the age of twelve.
Under the Treaty of 1866, reparations were due to the enslaved and native peoples. They gave them rocky rotten earth, infertile soil, and told them it was precious. Told them to be thankful. Like most things they give us to throw away, we turned it into progress. They found oil on their land.

Sarah became so wealthy Oklahoma legislation declared her White.
Stripped her of Blackness like Toby strangled Kunta.
Because Black girls can't handle money.
Might throw it away on freedom.
Might buy back husbands and fathers.
Might use it to blackmail the rapists and we can't have that.
If Black girls have money they must be White.
Like white lights over Black bodies on Black streets with empty hands and broken chests.
White like . . . administrative leave.
White like . . . not guilty.
White like . . . community service.
White like . . . the lilies they lay on our caskets.
White like . . . the noise of bullets ringing in our ears.
White like . . . our knuckles when we try not to fight back, try not to resist arrest.

White like . . . them.

The absence of color is not enough.
White folks wanted to erase her culture.
Because kinky hair looks too much like revolution.
Gotta straighten things that fight back, spring back.
They must lay it down like dogs, like niggers.
With heat.
With water.
Train it to submit.
She must be one of them.

Sarah does not belong to them.
Sarah belongs to the broken earth we dug through to find
our roots.
She belongs to the cracked hands welcoming us after long
journeys home.
The oil that made her rich was Black for a mother-fucking
reason.
It sprouted from the ground like prayers to heaven.
Slick like mother tongues you can't understand.
Like the claps and stomps used to communicate without our
voices.
She was Black.
She is Black.
I will always remember her as Black.
Sarah is one of us.

This is a story. This is a story about young Black men and Black mothers. I wanted to show the shift from saving for one's future and being excited about a child growing up, to saving up for funeral expenses. I often fear having children because the world is so cruel to Black bodies. Although this is a story I created, I recognize this is real life for many parents, siblings, spouses, and loved ones who have to shift their world-views after a tragedy.

When College Funds Become Funeral Expenses

We've been preparing for this day since before you were born.
I remember the first time I felt you kick the bucket of my belly.
I put a quarter in a jar I named your future.
Could start a band with the way your future sang like church tambourines.
I know you were destined to leave.
Each wave of mourning sickness gave way to dollar bills.
Wrote my first check toward your future when I pushed you into this world.
Never filled out the memo line.
Wasn't sure exactly if I birthed a Black boy or a body bag.

I always knew you'd move on one day, become your own man.
Walk out the door and never come back.
I think all moms are afraid of their children leaving home.
Try hard to cover up the targets we raised.

We had to find you the perfect outfit.

Knew how much you loved purple.
Never could quite understand why.
You said it made you feel famous.
Reminded you of struggle and revolution.
Must have got that from your daddy.
Now you're the face of the revolution.

We bought you a fresh suit and shiny shoes.
You were ready.
I wasn't ready to see you like that.
Dressed you up so no one could see the chalk left from your outline.

I always hoped you'd go to Morehouse.
Now there is only more house where you used to be.
Imagined you flirting with Spellman girls.
Worrying about tests and skipping class
I never prepared for you to attend America's rite of passage for Black boys.
Thought we'd be applying for scholarships instead of life insurance claims.
Instead of cold church pews and my invitation to a new sorority, a legacy of Black mothers bonded by the exhale of a murdered boy.

Packing your room was the hardest.
Children don't realize how much of their soul they leave in their rooms.
Started to pick up your damn socks.
Never could manage to make it to the laundry basket.
Making your bed took an hour, couldn't make it right.
Wasn't right.
Never straight enough or tight enough.
Found myself on the floor.
Wearing your snapback.
Debate trophies circling me like salt.

Couldn't stop trying to wear you.
Trying to have you close again
Your room still isn't clean.

Your dad dealt with your leaving better.
I think he always knew you'd end up like this.
He barely made it out when he was your age.
Knew this was a part of growing up.
A part of raising a Black boy is planning to mourn a Black boy.
He doesn't talk about it much.
But I hear him cry in the morning when you two used to play
basketball before school.

We always set four plates at the table.
Me, your dad, and your brother Trey.
I worry that you're not eating.
Wasting away all skin and bones in there.
Not sure if I hope you'll come home for the holidays or . . .
If we can imagine a meal without you.

You know we've been adding to your brother's future, same
as you.
I almost hope we never have to use it.
I don't know if I can bear another transfer of funds.
Another shift from college applications to death certificates.
I am barely holding on.
Praying he can escape pipelines from my womb to prison or
back to dirt.
Are we saving for his future or his death?
Now when I shake his future, it sounds like shells hitting the
ground instead of church tambourines.
So I keep writing checks for his fund.
Each time he tells me he got pulled over, was followed in a
store, or harassed at school, I write a check.
Every time he excels in math, wins an award, smiles, and laughs,
I write another check and I still keep the memo line blank

I Love You

I've been meaning to tell you I love you.
Instead, I bit my lip and cage the orchestra tuning in my mouth.
Fearing you'd hear cacophony when I speak.
Every time my tongue begins to play the concert of my desire,
I hesitate.
I've never said I love you first, even though you give me so
many reasons to say it. . .

When I feel insecure and want to cover my body in shameful
words.
You whisper antidotes over my tortured mind like ancestral
chants.
I want to tell you then.

I want to tell you as foreplay.
Seduce you into singing my praises.
Make you hard-pressed to ignore the hook of my song.
Use my wet tongue to whistle our favorite tune.
Collaborate and reciprocate my melodies.

I want to tell you in our intimacy.
My arched back is this body breaking from holding in the
phrasing.
My moans are ghosts escaping in search of their lost lovers.
Our bodies, synchronized movement of sound.

I want to tell you in the empty spaces.
When I press my ear to your chest and rap to the beats of your existence.

The biggest reason you gave me to tell you when I couldn't fight the feeling.
You looked at me with symphonic eyes and you whispered in my ear.
"It's Sunday, and Fat Shack has half-priced wings."
I lost it, became free-form jazz.
I wanted to scream "I love you."
Stand on my chair and make Tom Cruise blush.
Declare my undying love, my earth-shattering desire for chicken wings . . . I mean you.

I knew then I loved you.
Our ancestors were lovers separated by auction blocks only to find each other in our arms.
It was you, it has always been you.
Facilitated by Frank's hot sauce and fried chicken wings.
I knew I wanted to say all these things.
Become lighthouse.
Find the right moment to shine truth on the emotions ebbing inside.
You unlocked a piece of me that was yearning.
Transformed my body into a temple worth praying to.
Thank God that I found a place that has discount chicken wings.
Well, I mean thank God I found you.
It made me love the thought of you.
I began dreaming of our lives together.
We'd speak power against injustice.
Be Black power.
Be Black love.
Raise our fists and shake them at kids on our lawn.
Becoming old and remembering only each other.

Losing touch with reality and being grounded by your voice.
This . . . Hot wings . . . Half price.
You make me want to break my tradition.
Become maverick and tell you, I love you first.

Celestial Symphony

Did you know the planets have unique sounds?
I wonder what our hearts sound like orbiting each other.
The resonance of our souls colliding exists across the galaxy.
Could we be the big bang?
Maybe our metaphysical music is the soundtrack of creation.

Writer's Block

Figure out what you're holding instead of your pen.

Nature's Masterpiece

Wake up to sunrise streaked across canvas skies.
Art does not need paint.

This poem was years in the making. I have worked with youth for the majority of my life, and one of the recurring conversations I had was about smoking weed and creativity. The youth I worked with would tell me smoking made them more creative, less critical of their work, and more relaxed. I would tell them they can activate the same creativity and relaxed criticism without the use of weed. At the core of the conversation, young people wanted to be creative without getting bogged down with insecurity. I started to consider writing a poem about weed as creativity, where the process of smoking was actually the writing process.

Smokey Poems

When asked if you want to get high, say yes.
Rip a page from an old notebook full of confessions and catharsis.
Grab a bag of creativity you keep hidden. Smell it, tickle your nose with budding possibilities. The scent of your words lingers.

Pack a generous amount of your imagination. Lick the edge of the page, let the line run across your tongue like a dull blade. Remember how far you've come and all the times you choose paper and pen to dull your pain instead of a razor.

Roll it tight. Don't let any part of your ability go to waste. We are in the business of using every ounce of your potential.

Cradle your masterpiece in the corner of your mouth. Grab a lighter. Ignite your words and watch them catch fire. Notice the letters lifting on the rolled page and be reborn. See how your stories take shape in the smoke. The spirits of poetry dance for your amusement in the air.

Breathe deep and inhale. Fill your lungs with sonnets, haikus, free verse, and prose. You will cough, this is normal. Your body is reminding you that it's okay to let things go, that releasing is just as beautiful and necessary as retaining.

Now pass. Allow others to be filled with your literary language. Invite them into your mind. Make them witness the way poetry has saved you. Their experience will be different. The spirits will dance to a new beat in the air, but it is all connected.

The effects of your words will happen gradually, slowing down time and motion. Isn't that what good poetry is supposed to do, grant you permission from Father Time to run a line back and really listen?

Each puff provides clarity. The ability to see someone else's perspective. Imagine being in a room full of smokey poems and seeing clearly for the first time.

Your poetry is healing relief from the chronic pain of oppression, marginalization, and repression. A doorway to rest and rejuvenation.

Your poetry is a Schedule 1 drug. So powerful the government wants to regulate your voice, knows how influential your stories can be.

When you come to the end of your message and the flames kiss your lips, lick them, taste the remnants of your expression. Give thanks you saw your stories transform before you. Shake off the ashes of your suffering. Suffocate the embers and begin again.

A Seat at the Table
A Poetry Movement Piece with Jasmine Dillavou

From the desk of White privilege:

"You are cordially invited to take a seat at the table. Our once-closed society has opened, reluctantly.

There is enormous pressure to integrate, to align with the times.

Between you and me, this is an infringement of our rights, a reduction of our freedoms. This old boys' club is our history and our heritage.

But you, my beautiful exotic princess, are our solution. We believe you are the perfect fit.

You'll find your place at the end of the table. This is a probationary period, but don't be afraid, it's not the probation you're used to, no officers will be involved.

You'll sit behind this wall. You'll be invited to the full table in due time. We have to make sure we can trust you. We must protect our culture from criminals, rapists, and thugs, you know the like.

We've found bootstraps are the best way to make it over the wall quicker, and we know you are so good at climbing.

We have no seats to spare. There is an expectation you come with a seat. Were you not informed? Our members come with gold-plated, velvet-cushioned thrones with a pearl inlay. Most of us are born with it, others inherit it from our fathers.

You do know who your father is, right?

I see you come empty-handed. Unprepared. Ill-equipped to take your seat.
Figures you wouldn't be up to standard.

How do you expect us to welcome you when you don't even have a chair? Remember you are taking up a seat of a deserving member. Always remember you are taking up our space and our air.

A pity

Luckily we have building materials. We know your kind are hardworking, always happy to steal a job with affirmative action.

We have scraps of lumber, molded and warped. Rusty nails. Shards of glass. Build it while we watch. We get off on your manual labor.

Although you'd be a voting member, we had to compromise. Make sure we still retain control, so your vote will only be counted as three-fifths of a person.

You're one of the lighter ones, so that counts in your favor. You can pass for one of us. Aren't you grateful for that privilege? You're half, right?

Half White.
Half American.
Half normal.
Half palatable.

We have our obvious reservations about your race, but we are deeply concerned about your uterus. About your predisposition for hysteria. We are afraid you might bleed and ruin the carpet. Might make irrational decisions while seated at the table.

We think you could cause us to waver. We men have needs and your presence will make us
Hungry
Thirsty
Uncontrollable for such a spicy fiery woman.

I suggest you dress plainly so as not to cause a stir, as not to cause your own undoing. Legs and chest covered, hair straightened and professional. No makeup. No hoops.

Then there is the trouble of your name. We appreciate how easy it sits on our tongues. It's not difficult for our throats to muster and yet . . .
There is a problem with the board list. When your name is listed, it's not easy to show you are . . . exotic. Isn't that what this is all about? To show we did it. We let you in. Gave you a seat.

So we'll assign you a nickname, an ethnic name. A name that jumps off our board list, and says colored, like Maria, Felicia, Lee, or Cheyenne. One of your names we can actually pronounce.

It's best for everyone if you work on your English. You are very articulate. You almost sound like a native. But there is a hint, a tone, an accent that is too much like foreigner, too much like alien to our ears. We'll provide you with a tutor. Extinguish any flames of your ancestors living on your tongue.

We'll make a member out of you yet. All you have to do is take a seat at our table."

The response from the desk of Women of Color:

We disrespectfully decline your tasteless offer.

Although you believe you are doing us a favor, we have never needed nor wanted a seat at your table.

A table that was forged from stolen land and resources of indigenous people. Seats built from the blood and sweat of brown bodies. Stuffed with cotton picked by slaves who bear your last name. All on a foundation of the emotional and physical labor of women of color.

You call yourselves progressive when you have barely taken a step further than your forefathers. You hide your oppression and misogyny in bylaws, while actively enacting racism.

We are seats unto ourselves. Our table is laid and protected by our ancestors. Magic and power are our inheritance.

We are fortified by the strength of women who have bled while handling their shit.
We will nurture the home in our mouths, the accents, and the language that connects us. Use those flames to burn down a system created against us.

We will take up your space, your air, and your energy and claim it for those who have been silenced. We are not your stolen trophies and diversity hires. We are exceptionally excellent, educated, and essential in every space we exist in.

I cordially invite you to sit down, shut up, and be humble. Bear witness to our board of directors.

Watch as we prepare the table we have built and blessed. Know we will invite in perpetuity all who have been oppressed by the desk of White privilege to take their rightful seat.

Boundaries are Love

I can't do everything.
I have the right to say no.
Not every opportunity is meant to be taken .
I can be whole without a full schedule.
I deserve to take time for myself.

Daily Practice

This is a reminder.
Drink water.
Flirt with your reflection.
Sleep.
Stand in awe of your body.
Eat.
Make love to yourself.
Wash your face.
Whisper sweet nothings to your soul.
Take time off.
Brag about your survival.
Seek help.
Acknowledge how far you've come.
This is a reminder.

This poem was inspired after learning how string cheese was created!
Inspiration is everywhere. In the most basic terms, mozzarella cheese is
stretched and pulled while being heated up to 140 degrees. At this tem-
perature, the milk proteins move and change and become stretchy. This
process made me think of what being a girl felt like, especially around
self-esteem and puberty. Girls are told to dislike themselves—be better,
prettier, nicer, be perfect—and they get stretched in all these directions,
sometimes without realizing it. I wanted this poem to reinforce that we have
always been enough, and we get to decide who we become and who we are.

You Are Enough

Girls, this is a reminder of who you are, warriors in this world.
They think we are unworthy. They call themselves doubt.
They proclaim power is determined by our gender.
But we know the truth, we've been fighting monsters under
our beds for years
with our secret weapon.
Our strength was never questioned until one night when they
came for us.
They planted seeds of deception in minds only beginning to
learn to love our bodies.
They told us we're not beautiful.
They told us we'll never be smart enough.
Strong enough.
Loud enough.
We will never be enough.
For him
For her.
For ourselves.
We become convinced we are broken beyond repair.

Begin peeling away pieces of our bodies to sacrifice to a deity we created out of piles of lost self-esteem.
Sparked with the friction of wanting to love ourselves and being told it'll never be enough.
In the eyes of the flame, we shrink.
We recoil and are bound so tight that the fibers of our existence merge into a form that bears no resemblance to our soul.
We start to listen to the whispers that tell us to give up.

But this is our declaration.
I dare you to cut the threads they told you to sew over your mouth and scream **I AM BEAUTIFUL. I AM ENOUGH.** The vibrations of our voices ring loud and suffocate the once-engulfing fire.
Your voice is the remedy for a disease they created and spread.
You are the most valuable person in your life.
Peel back the layers of your charred heart.
Give life the opportunity to showcase the strength beating inside.
Because you are alive, the secret weapon we've been holding all along.
Put your hand to your heart and feel.
Feel every beat.
Every word.
Decipher the Morse code that your body aches for you to know.
You are love.
Each heartbeat signals dots and dashes to tell you that before there was hurt and hate and lies, we've been fighting monsters under our beds day and night.
To the girls who conquered their fears.
To the girls who walked through the world proud and strong.
That metronome song is a reminder of who you are.
Your battle cry.
Because as long as your heart beats, you will always be enough.

Order of Operations

Love yourself.
Forgive yourself.
Take care of this temple body you call home.
There is power in the way you smile at your figure in the morning.

Angela Davis spoke at the University of Colorado, Colorado Springs, and shared the idea that hope does not naturally exist; instead it is generated. As I listened to her words, the imagery of a bubble machine appeared. Each bubble a signal for others to hope deeply and frequently.

Hope

Hope is a bubble machine within each of us. We generate hope. At times there is an abundance of bubbles cascading around us.

When we are hopeless we walk through the soft bubbles of our community to find hope again.

The Pledge of Allegiance is weird. It wasn't until I was older that I started to think about this practice. Me, a young Black girl pledging allegiance to the country that stole, tortured, raped, and killed my ancestors. It's wild! As I was working through this discovery, I thought about what I would want to pledge allegiance to, and I decided I wanted to honor myself. This poem is my daily affirmation to care for myself, honor my emotions, and love who I am and who I am becoming!

Pledge

I pledge allegiance to the honoring of every form of this body
and to my ancestors for whom I stand.
One goddess.
Under love.
Indivisible.
With equity and equality for all.

I am committed to the protection and maintenance of my
temple.
I will lay offerings at my feet.
I will love and cherish this body in perpetuity.
I promise to listen and tend to my needs.
I will respect and maintain my boundaries.
Only speak love and kindness over my body.

I dedicate myself to the softening of rough skin and the protection of melanin.
I stand guard in defense of my heart.
I am at the beck and call of my mental health.

I will nurse the wounds of the past and practice radical self-acceptance.

Every night I will light candles in the catacombs of my trauma. Honor the parts of me that have suffered and nourish the survivor I've become.
I will accentuate my curves.
Touch my scars often as a reminder that I have overcome and healed.

I will openly celebrate and announce my love for this body.
I will walk with my head held high.
Feel the beauty of my curly 4c hair.
I will allow myself a full range of emotions without judgment or fear.
I will smile at my reflection and treat myself with respect.
I will diligently remind myself that I am enough and always have been.
I pledge allegiance to me.

PART 2

Sometimes we write for ourselves and sometimes we write for others who need it the most. Why risk not impacting someone's life by not sharing your words? This is the advice I give anyone nervous to share their work or create for others. I invite you to read the gifts I have the honor of presenting to my communities.

This was a commission for Colorado Springs Utilities for MLK Day in 2018. Stereotypes are frequently a source of inspiration for my work. For this poem, I addressed the stereotype that Black people are loud and leaned into the idea. Instead of combating the stereotype, I wanted to show exactly why we are loud and why it's important we continue to be loud. This is one of my signature poems. I'm proud this poem is one people remember me for, and I hope it inspires others to use their voice and never stay silent.

Defy Silence

People have often called us Black folks loud, boisterous, and thundering. Our laugh crackling cackles and exuberant exalting are deemed uncouth in certain spaces.

Our voices cacophony to most ears, jazz to those with seasoned pallets. We turn up to turbulent bass levels. We bump Tupac, blast Toni Braxton, and crank up Billie Holiday. We provide front-row concerts to the entire neighborhood.

We do not know how to mourn quietly. We wail and scream in hopes our voices are resurrection enough for the buried. Our voices are reincarnations of our ancestors' prayers.

Even our whispers are seismic.

There is no distinguishing between inside and outside voices. As caged birds now free, we sing too loud and too often, making up for years of oppressed silence.

Being loud means we are alive. It means we have found a way to survive and are celebrating.

We are defying darkness with demonstrative declarations of love. Dr. King once said, "Our lives begin to end the day we become silent about things that matter."

Which is to say, Black Lives Matter.
Which is to say, Black Voices Matter.

When textbooks silence slavery and call it a cultural exchange, we get louder.

When Black girls go missing and the news reports a cat stuck in a tree instead of her name, instead of her picture, we get louder.

When Black men are murdered and their killers are called heroes, we get louder.

We have been loud for centuries and we will continue to raise our voices against injustice. We will dedicate our harmonies as an homage to Rev. Dr. Martin Luther King Jr. A leader so powerful his impact is still reverberating in our ears.

Do not think this poem is about the volume of our voices.

This is about the power of speaking up in a world that is expecting you to remain silent.

Will you join us and be loud?
Will you defy silence with your voice?

As you read a book, your mind creates a whole new world. Sometimes, books give us the demographic information of the characters, and other times, we have to fill it in with our imagination. I came to the realization that I usually made the main characters White with an average build, both things I am not. It was a hard reality to face that my imagination was colonized; given the open landscape of my mind, I didn't allow myself to be in the narrative. I believe it all starts with our imagination and expanding our minds to create worlds where we are the main characters.

Decolonizing Imagination

Imagine the main character of a story.
See her running through an open field. Her skin shimmering in the sun, her hair a riptide of waves in the wind. Laughter spirals from her lips to heaven in between songs her grandmother taught her. Awaiting an embrace from her partner.

What does she look like?
What color is her skin?
What texture is her hair?
What language does she sing?
Who is her partner?

We fill in the gaps with a single story, with the most common idea of main characters.
Often denying ourselves full representation even in our imagination.

We do not do this innately. This practice is learned and instilled from the books we read, the shows we watch, and the art we experience.

The content matters.

It allows us to be seen and validated in the literature. Find ourselves in the pages of a hardback book where the main character reflects a part of our identity. Where the story addresses the struggles and joys of our lived experiences.

Books are a portal to curated worlds that have been saving readers for centuries, opening perspectives and connections. As we read we can grow in understanding and empathy.

But what if we didn't have to fill in the gaps?
What if the books were already celebrations of diversity and equity?
What if you could feel represented and safe by the stories you read?

What if, her deep brown skin shimmered in the sun, as her thick coarse hair waved across her head like a riptide. Singing a Spanish song her grandmother taught her while she clung to her side in the kitchen as a child. She will forever smell fresh chilis when she sings. The embrace of her wife feels like coming home.

What if we didn't have to force ourselves to fit in the narrative?
What if we made stories of our own where we are the main characters?

Let's create and promote inclusive stories.
Honor experiences and content outside of historical standards. With every turn of a page, we decolonize our imagination and diversify our world.

The National Alliance for Mental Illness (NAMI) Colorado Springs commissioned me to create a poem for their NAMIWalks event. I explored the question, what does community mental health look like without any infrastructure? If there were no therapists, social workers, or community mental health programs, how would we support each other? What does basic human support of mental health look like? This poem reveals that we heal in relationships and we need each other.

Finding Myself

I see you in all the ways you show up.
The authentic expression.
The unraveling and coming undone when the tempest replaces sunlight.

I see you in the eye of the storm.
Behind the dysregulation and disorganization, you are a human trying their best.
I am unafraid of swirling catharsis.
I will sit with you.
Hold your hand through it all.
Even when it feels impossible to stay connected, I will not let go.

I see you across the turgid sea in boats of protective factors.
Honoring the ways we fight the waves to exist.
Warriors in our own right.
Some fight with words and others with elixirs.
Drenched and worn we emerge in tomorrow's sun to survive again.

We hold different levels of waterlogging in our battle bodies.
We know it is heavy for us all.
You see me as another weatherworn traveler.
We acknowledge in each other the ways we are broken and blessed.
Kissed by saltwater and fatigue.

I see you on this journey.
Healing is not linear.
We are ocean waves and riptides.
Spiraling and arching into and out of our trauma.
Awaiting the integration.
Awaiting the stillness of mind and body.
There is beauty in the ebbing and flowing.
The process of navigating rough water.

Being seen means we recognize ourselves in each other.
I see you have become strong and capable from battles.
Let me hold what you've been carrying.
Heavy hearts.
Exhausted minds.
Anxious bodies.
I will bear witness.
Scream to match the pitch of your pain.
Sit in the silence.
Nurture the tears.
Become container.
Validate the storms we all come from.

I see you in your revolutionary joy.
In the beauty of humanity.
The way your laugh ripples across the still water.
I see your sunrise smile dance across your face.
I see you at your best.
On smooth currents and starlight paths where progress is straight ahead.

You are holistic and dynamic.
We hold both.
The battles and the liberation.
The distress and the pleasure.

The storms will always pass and may return another day.
We remain, as does the ocean, powerful and resilient.
Undefined by each day's weather.
Amongst challenges and chaos.
Through the break in the clouds for sunlight to return.
We find ourselves reflected in each other.

Black boys and men deserve to feel all of their emotions, to cry, and to heal from past traumas. For survival, Black people have to hide their emotions, but just because you hide them doesn't mean they go away. Generational curses can be broken by naming the need to emote, cry, scream, and in this case, heal from childhood trauma.

Salt

Peace to the Black boys drowning in their own tears.
Tasting salt and calling it poison.
Naming it shame.
Suffocating under the oceans of their catharsis.
Not knowing seas of salt give us buoyancy.
Allows bodies overflowing with trauma, heavy from kept secrets and repressed truths, the experience of weightlessness.
The involuntary exhale when someone believes you.
Know you are worth believing.

Black boys, keep crying.
Cry until you have enough water to drown your abusers.
Black boys you are life raft.
Are sailboat.
Are cruise ship.
Black boys, cry.
Black boys, float.
Black boys, survive.

Strength to the Black men surviving in the desert of their own wasteland past.
Never told they carry life preserves in their voice.
Drowned a thousand salty deaths.
Learning to cut out their tear ducts is the same as healing.
Taught their kin the danger moisture brings.
How salt water burns open wounds.
Instructed them to build homes in arid landscapes.
Creating generations of dry mouths.
Cracked lips and stories caught in throats, trying to scratch their way out.

Cry, Black men.
Your tears are long overdue.
Allow years of generational drought to be nourished by your emotional release.
Black men you are gardener.
Are irrigation systems.
Are spring rain.
Black men, cry.
Black men, grow.
Black men, heal.

This piece was commissioned for a women's conference called PowHer focused on gathering and supporting women of color, allies, and change agents across industries. The strength and resilience of mother nature inspired the comparison of women of color to flowers and plants. Despite barriers to access and complex systems of oppression women of color continue to exist, thrive, and pave the wave for others to do the same.

Concrete Revolution

Mother Nature has never been stopped by the concrete work of man.

We see moss, sunflowers, and even trees grown from cement slabs in harsh conditions.

Flourishing, propagating, and blooming in environments that did not appear to hold a garden under its compact bases.

We women of color are cracking asphalt, shifting blacktops, and disrupting sidewalk supremacy with our existence.

There is no matter strong enough to keep us suppressed.

Our voices are rose-petal pedagogy. Teaching future generations of the oasis we hold on our tongues. Effortlessly powerful, spiraled in sharp activism.

Climbing vines of determination reach higher and higher in every endeavor.

Our seedling bodies bloom wherever we are planted. Even in the rough and cracked soil, we become grapevine resilient.

This is not magic, though we are magically made. This is the work of ancestral dividends. Watered by perseverance, joy, and passion.

Each of us is cultivating gardens in our communities where once it was believed nothing could grow.

We are the fertilizer and the harvest!

We are jungles, forests, meadows, and botanical gardens.

May we create landscapes in our image.

Watch each of us become conservatories. We are filling in the gaps with the brilliance of our intersectionality.

Stand in awe of our strength and the depth our roots will go to nourish each other.

All it takes is one flower to crack the system, to create change.

All it takes is one weed to grow where it isn't wanted to disrupt the norm.

All it takes is women of color existing, piercing adversity with the spark of your bloom to start a revolution.

This was a commission from Colorado Springs Utilities for MLK Day. Water is a powerful element and often underestimated. Writing this, I imagined—what if all of the marches, protests, and demonstrations were depicted as rushing water? The impact of everyone coming together in a roaring wave would be tremendous; it would wash away barriers and create new paths. The image of the Colorado River creating the Grand Canyon was a huge influence on my conceptualization of activism.

Water

We are gathered here today to make history.
To start a revolution our ancestors were killed for.
Continue the work of dynamic leaders before us.
Our presence is nothing short of extraordinary.
When they write about this day, call us water.
Each of us a drop, making ripples in the lakes we call home.
Often underestimated.
Called annoying, the leaky faucet, the broken pipe.
Always voicing our opinions and standing for what's right.
Together we are swirling bodies of water.
Rivers of resistance.
Oceans of oppressed survivors.

Do you know the power of a million drops of water?
How the Colorado River carved the Grand Canyon?
Eroded rock deep and slowly.
The way tides can destroy beach cliffs, sink ships and nations in one wave.
Hurricanes are just drops of water propelled by the wind that can uproot cities.

Do not underestimate our droplet bodies.
Together we can wear down foundations and statues and systems erected to hold us back.
We will teach generations the value of water.
Hold it sacred and revered.
How even a drop can start to make a change in a stagnant environment.
Show how monumental it is when we come together.

You can not break us down.
We are resilient.
If you try to cut us we will continue to flow.
If you place obstacles in front of us we will divert into new paths.
If you contain us we will leak.

Today we are gathered together to turn the faucets on, let the pipes burst, and destroy the dam
Activate our activism.
Watch our bodies in unison, like water pouring into the streets, as a reminder that there is work to do, that there is change afoot.
Each step we take will leave a path for others to follow.
A deep groove in the system until we carve a new canyon so grand the walls are etched in equity and equality.
For those who are not convinced of their buoyancy, remember we are mostly water.
When we chant love not hate, the song of our voices vibrates through the water in our bodies and we literally become music.
We become fierce activism.

Call us water.
Call us activists.
Never underestimate our power when we come together and flow.

This was a commission for the Boettcher Foundation Fellowship program. There were three poetry performances and each artist was assigned a topic about leadership. My theme was about being a good neighbor. I was inspired by our ability to know so much about the world and often know so little of our neighborhoods and community.

It's a Beautiful Day in the Neighborhood

It has been said, we were never meant to know everything happening in the world.
We were always meant to know what was happening with our neighbors and community.

It is far more likely you can share the names, ages, and current relationship status of every cast member of The White Lotus than the name of your neighbor.

It is far more likely people will notice if Brittany Spears stops making twirling dance videos for months than if their neighbor hasn't picked up their newspaper for two weeks and their car hasn't moved.

It is far more likely we know about the deep loss of those in a recent publicized tragedy, than if your neighbor is grieving the loss of his young daughter.

The ability to know and see the world is a gift, a generational advancement, but we must not lose the generational blessing that is community.

To be a neighbor and check in, be curious, and be courageous in our support.

Being a neighbor is not about the proximity to others in a home, but rather the ability to make any day beautiful by caring for each other. Showing up fully and adding to the brilliance of the community.

It's a beautiful day in the neighborhood when I know more about my neighbors than I do the rest of the world.
When I know the names of the dogs and cats on my street.
When I can smile and wave at the family across the way as I leave for work.
When my neighbor notices I'm stuck in the snow and offers to dig me out.
The beautiful days are when I feel like I belong in my community.

It's a beautiful day in the neighborhood
When Black Lives are creating symphonies, laughing overtures conducting movements of friends swaying to the sounds of strong voices and connections.

It's a beautiful day in the neighborhood when I can name the Black-owned restaurants and businesses in my city.
When I see flags reminding me that my life always matters.
When Black elders are neighbors and we know each other's names.

It's a beautiful day in the neighborhood
When queerness is protected and celebrated.
When neighbors introduce themselves with their name and pronouns, permission slips for others to do the same.

It's a beautiful day when who you love is not a prerequisite for acceptance.
Where neighbors show up authentically for each other and there is safety in joy, expression, and gender identity.

It's a beautiful day in the neighborhood when accessibility is at the forefront of the community, when ramps and elevators are not afterthoughts but intentional acts of respect.
Where limits are just opportunities for creative reconstruction and action.

It's a beautiful day in the neighborhood when multiple languages are rising like steam and the comfort of mother tongues is warm and loud.
It's a beautiful day when the smell of food from recipes that have traveled generations, oceans, and skies permeates from backyards and kitchens.
It is a beautiful day when diversity transforms from existing in a space to knowing you belong.

Won't you be the neighbor who helps make sure we know more about each other than we do the world?

We were always meant to be in community, to care for one another, and to grow in relationships.

Make today a beautiful day in OUR neighborhood!

This poem is in honor of the Grandmother of Juneteenth, Opal Lee, and her work to make Juneteenth a federal holiday. Juneteenth is about joy and freedom, and even more than that, it is about joy and freedom that was two and a half years overdue. This freedom day also recognizes liberation from the horrific acts of enslavement and the desire for those who didn't get to see freedom come to feel the joy through our celebrations.

Juneteenth

I say "good morning" to freedom.
Welcome a blushing sunrise with a deep inhale.
Filling lungs with enough air to carry me into tomorrow.
Exhale and paint the sky with a breath of affirmation that a new day has come.
The day we've been waiting for, praying for, living for.
She has arrived in brilliance.
How I wish she could have warmed the faces of ancestors turning toward God in hopes of flying away.
This day is a reminder, even caged birds still know how to fly.
This day is the remembrance of our ability to soar.
Practicing the weightlessness that comes with liberation.
The inertia of muscle memory falling into place and claiming all the times we've taken flight.
The courage to take one step outside of plantations and run under North Star protection.
The gall to drink long and slowly from water fountains under "White only" signs.

The power of sitting steadfastly on bus seats and diner stools, while hate rained down like hellfire around you.

The fire to advocate for Black lives to walk, run, sleep, drive, and exist without fear of violence.

The strength of marching for progress two and a half miles at a time to honor this day.

Every action is a reclaiming of the open sky we came from.

Mark this day as the culmination of voices carried on the breeze like sheet music.

Wind-song equality and advocacy in every language known and lost.

Let the world hear we will always fight for freedom, ours and yours.

Bring the sun and bring the light on days once dark.

Revolution and renaissance burn bright after suffering.

We are cause for celebration, the song, dance, music, and laughter.

All smiles and jubilee.

Freedom is not a silent occurrence, it is loud and forthcoming.

It is deafening and fills the sky with only the sound of our creation.

Hear the crack of thunder, the roar of the wind, and the buzz of sunshine, knowing it is our soundtrack for emancipation.

Rejoice until the day turns to night.

Revel under the moonlight like your joy will keep the day from turning to tomorrow.

Heal in relationship and teach others how independence feels alongside a community.

Our celebration is the air allowing us to fly, soar, climb, and welcome freedom's tomorrow.

Fannie Mae Duncan and the Cotton Club are a huge part of Colorado Springs history. I was asked to create a poem for Fannie Mae in preparation for her statue installation in Colorado Springs. Her slogan was "Everybody Welcome," and I wanted this phrase to be at the forefront of this poem. It was important to explain why she said "everybody welcome" and what she was facing every time she spoke those words aloud. She is an incredible figure in our city, and as a Black woman, a powerful inspiration. This was one of my first poems about a historical figure, and it sparked a love for poetry as historic text.

Everybody Welcome

You are not welcome here!
We don't like the way your skin resembles fertile earth.
Reminds us, even if we try to bury you, your seedling bodies
will bloom.

You are not welcome here!
We hate the way your hair curls toward heaven.
A sign of royalty and godliness we are not ready to accept.

You are not welcome here!
We don't think your kind belongs in this town.
Find it easier to assert dominance when we have chased and
killed the others and named them inferior.

You are not welcome here!
We don't think you deserve to breathe our air.
Drink our water.
Eat our food.
Wouldn't dare have you live in our homes.

Your rested bodies have too much potential to start revolutions, so we must keep you tired and awake

You are not welcome here!
We can't stand how you can make music in the breakbeats, the empty spaces, with hands and mother tongues.
Reminds us of the humanity, culture, and life we actively try to deny you.
You are not welcome here!

To this she replied, everybody welcome!
Fannie Mae Duncan is jazz soul priestess.
Made her home between the lines of sheet music and upright bass strings.
Reverberated her message.
Hypnotized onlookers and made them activists.
Turned segregation and racism into scats.
Deconstructed the laws and handed them back as music drenched in culture and ancestry.
She knew the value of unique sounds coming together as one.
Jam sessions are messy and beautiful in the most powerful way.
Jazz band cannot be homogeneous, it needs the diversity of a rich tenor, an earthy baritone, a bright soprano, and a steady beat.

She welcomed free-form jazz, the offbeats, the slant rhymes, and the rough voices.
She knew change and revolution are not perfect or pristine.
Set her metronome to feet marching in the streets and every rest a moment of silence for the lives lost in the fight.
Fannie Mae saged the Cotton Club with equality and equity in every corner, and bodies could join in unison to sway and bop to sounds that tingle our spines and arouse our minds.
She blessed every doorway as legends graced the stage.
Saw depression in the blues and intergenerational trauma in the bones of piano chords, and provided therapy in the way of an audience.

She made legends out of the patrons, she made a legend of
Colorado Springs.
Brought music to drown out the sounds of oppression and
police brutality.
Integrated her beats.
Decriminalized the art of existing in the same room.

Her influence in every word of this poem.
I can feel her at nightclubs when the bass runs through my
body and replaces my heartbeat.
She left us with this teaching, one Dr. King referenced.
Darkness cannot drive out darkness, only light can do that.
Hate cannot drive out hate, only love can.
She refused to stand down.
Stood tall like Black women often do in the face of adversity.
Composed a song of inclusion to be our anthem.
She offered up love to every statement of aggression and
cease and desist.
She offered up light and said, everybody welcome.

To the Black dignitaries worn from trips across the country
not allowed in hotels in the Springs, she replied, everybody
welcome.

To the interracial couple wanting solace in their love, tired
of hiding their relationship from hateful eyes, she replied,
everybody welcome.

To the Black people of Colorado Springs turned away from
White spaces and feeling invisible, she replied, everybody
welcome.

To the jazz lovers, the night goers, the midnight tokers, she
replied, everybody welcome.

She replied and continues to reply to anyone who seeks her wisdom and learns her lessons.
She reminds us, everybody welcome.
No qualifiers or prerequisites.
There is only a coming home, a returning to love, to light, to jazz, to the Cotton Club.
A reminder that we have always been welcome.

For a local celebration of International Women's Day I played with the idea of the future. What the future would look like, how women would feel about themselves, the dreams they'd have, and the world they'd inherit. In many ways this is a love letter of hope to the next generation.

Our Future

The future is Female.
is Woman
is Femme
is Trans.
is Black and Brown.
Is, is, is.
The future is our gift to generations of women known and unknown.
We are the stewards of a landscape we have been instructed to protect.
To tend to and grow so that we may produce a harvest that will fruit and bloom and propagate in perpetuity.
Care for Mother Nature as a fellow woman, honor her, and see to her healing.
This is a sisterhood.
Every accomplishment, every advancement, and every vote is powerful beyond measure.
Our hands will hold open doors of opportunity.

Reach back to the community to make sure we pull forward woman after woman after woman to stand beside us.

Our voices are affirmation spells.

Finding their way to every woman who has ever doubted her worth.

We will make a narrative where we are strong, capable, powerful, and brilliant.

Loud enough to drown out the looped rhetoric of insecurity society indoctrinates in us.

Our bodies will know how beautiful they are.

Our revolution will start with ourselves.

We will honor and walk confidently in every shape, size, shade, and ability.

We will take up space and teach others this ritual is our birthright.

Practice expanding and claiming equality and equity along the way, clutched between fingers turned into a fist, raised as we empower others to fight for justice.

When the time is ready, we will unclench, unfold, and present the future to those taking up the charge.

Offer a legacy of women who have sacrificed, laughed, cried, and cheered to make sure the future is there to inherit.

We know the future will have access to healthcare and body autonomy.

The future will have strong and soft women in leadership.

The future will have an environment suitable for women to grow, live, thrive, and play.

The future will be a gift from us today.

This was my first poem commissioned for the Women of Influence award, which celebrates women in Colorado Springs who have significantly impacted and influenced their communities. I was asked along with two other women to read poems to start out the night. I imagined looking in a mirror in times of doubt or distress and seeing hundreds of women behind me, from family to friends to mentors and leaders. I wanted this poem to honor the struggles of being a woman and femme in the world, and reinforce that we are not alone and we never will be alone.

To the Woman Who Has Ever Felt Alone

To the woman who has ever felt alone, there is a community of strong women behind you.
In every boardroom. Classroom. House. Battlefield. Courthouse.
Salaried, hourly, minimum-wage job. We are there.
When you look in the mirror, see us standing behind you.
We are celebrating your successes and singing affirmations to combat self-doubt.
We coven of influential women, circle you in protection, salt, sage, and empathy,

In the morning we cleaned and laid out your armor.
We will dress you for battle.
Soften your heart.
Tighten your smile.
Fortify your spirit.
Anoint your shield.
We are soldiers in your army.

When you are treated unjustly, override your feelings lest anyone see you succumb to your emotions.

We will tell you to cry.
Baptize your checks with hot tears.
Be reborn in the catharsis of sorrow.

We are there when your opinion falls silent in the forest of male voices.
Breaking itself just to get the attention of the room.
We see and hear you.
We will spend time replanting you in earth.
Collecting the pieces you offered to the forest.
Reinforce you with iron support, love, and warmth.

Every time you swallow anger and smile through your teeth for fear of being called a bitch, for fear of being called aggressive or disruptive, lean on your community.
Scream to us, curse, yell, express your frustrations.
We will hold them.
Validate you are worthy to feel.
Provide space to be a human.

When you are the only woman at the table, imagine each empty space filled with us.
We Black women, Asian women, Latina women, indigenous women, women of color,
trans women, disabled women, fat women, queer women, poor women, old women, all women.
See yourself represented in us.
You are never alone.
Our collective consciousness will feed into you.
Your presence, although singular for now, will influence generations to come.

We ask you take up space.
Be big, bold, beautiful, and bountiful.
Spread your voice like men spread their legs on bus seats.
Walk into your power with your head high.

Fill a room with your presence.
Give birth to your ideas and nurture them into reality.
Make people know you will not be moved.
Your thick trunk is rooted in your ancestors' buried dreams.
You are the harvest they prayed for.
Collect yourself and reap the benefits of a thousand willing sacrifices.
Stand strong.
Stand for us.
Stand in the protection of the next influential woman who thinks she's alone.

Each year the King Center selects a theme for MLK Day. In 2022 the theme was "It Starts with Me: Shifting Priorities to Create the Beloved Community." I was invited to speak at MLK Day at Colorado College. All the speakers were the first in their field. I am the first Black woman to hold the title of Pikes Peak Region Poet Laureate. As a Black woman, I am usually the first to do a lot of things since I have lived, been educated in, and worked in predominantly White spaces. I have always looked at being the first as a huge accomplishment for oneself, but also as a road map for others to follow. I remember when Obama was elected president and I heard many people express excitement because we finally reached "equality." In response to this notion, a comedian said that in order for us to have equality, we'd need to have forty-four Black male presidents in a row. This has always stuck with me because being the first is great, but the big work is how do you make sure you're not the last.

It Starts with Us

When you are "the first," you become an ancestor in your own right.

You become history. Doing so disrupts the historical standards and representation of excellence.

When you are the first, you are cashing in on decades of hard work, advocacy, love, and joy from elders and community members before you.

When you are the first and represent marginalized identities, you are setting fire to a system that works tirelessly to oppress you. You are redefining the way generations will look at what you've done.

We are models of possibility.

Our existence is an affirmation for those who thought it was impossible to be the first.

The first to go to college.

The first to own a home.

The first in their field.

The first to represent their communities.

Being first is not only an inspiration but a placeholder for those who come next.

Your work will turn into a legacy.

So many of us are the direct results of the work and life of Dr. King. Of his unrelenting passion and drive for equity, justice, and peace. For some of us, he was the first Black leader that taught us we have a place in this work.

As we stand in the doors opened by leaders, activists, healers, and warriors before us, may we recognize and smile at the sound of voices being added to the narrative.

I am the first Black Poet Laureate of the Pikes Peak Region, and I can't wait to meet the twentieth.

I can't wait to read stories about the first Black, Brown, indigenous, person of color and all their accomplishments.

I can't wait to learn what you do.

But in order for this to happen, it has to start with us.

It starts with our innovation and passion to step into these roles.

You may be the first in your family to stand up for what you believe in.

You may be the first in your job to advocate for change.

You may be the first person to accomplish something never done before.

Your bravery and courage to start something new will lay down roots of trees that will continue to grow long after you're gone.

All it takes is you believing that your actions are powerful enough to birth a forest of possibilities.

All it takes is the faith that your voice is nourishment for a bountiful harvest.

All it takes is you planting the seed, knowing when you bloom, there will be a vibrant garden that follows.

Be the first, become an ancestor, become history, and inspire the next person to accomplish something great.

This poem was created for a project in which participants in an art performance stood on a plinth, the heavy base supporting a statue. It was a commentary on what society deems important enough to have as a statue and was meant to reclaim space for artists to have the spotlight. Black girls and women are always on my mind when I create. I played with the term "Black don't crack" and interpreted it in the sense that Black women have to regulate their emotions and expression for survival. I wrote this around the time Gale King did an interview with R. Kelly in which she was praised for her stoic nature and emotions as R. Kelly escalated during the interview. I hated that so much of the commentary was about Gale's reactions rather than condemning R. Kelly's behavior. Black women deserve to be angry, to be sad, to be everything they are. I want this poem to validate the way many Black women have felt, and to remind Black girls their emotions are beautiful and powerful.

Black Don't Crack

The saying goes Black don't crack.
We are told this is about our complexion. How melanin is the fountain of youth, our reparations in the form of immortality.
It is also about the way we Black women hold up the foundations of our emotions with a broken smile.
It's about the painted masks we wear for protection.
How to survive knowing our emotions are loaded guns
Society is waiting for us to start shooting, get hood, be ghetto.

Go ahead, Black girl.
Get mad.
Get loud.
Prove us right.
Make us hate you.
Justify our trigger fingers.
Better not catch you being angry, Black girl.
Wouldn't want people to feel scared, Black girl.

So we bridle our tongues.
Cage our anger, lest they call us bitch, nigger, cunt.
Might burn down systems with the heat of our fury.
Our mouths hold life and death on our tongues, and they can't
handle what our mouths do, so we swallow our emotions.
Let them take root in our bones until they crack us open,
crack under the weight of
Murder.
Rape.
Torture.
Slavery.
Sexism
Racism.
Crack, because Black women are three times more likely to
die of childbirth.
Crack, because Black trans women experience violence at
increased rates.
Crack, because the study of gynecology was built on the
experimentation of Black enslaved women.
Crack, because Henrietta Lacks's cells were stolen and used
to advance science.
Crack, because Black women weren't able to vote until 1965.
Crack, because Black women activists around the country are
turning up dead.
Crack, because Black mothers are in the business of burying
their Black sons.

This is enough for anyone to let slip, let rip the justifiable
anger, and burn shit down.
Of course, we are furious. The list of our grievances is long
and bloodied, but we can't crack, so we smile.

Because Black girls don't get sad.
We don't succumb to the drowning of depression.
Since Black people are afraid of water, right?

Don't cry, Black girl.
Wouldn't want people to think you're weak.
Wouldn't want people to think you're not happy.
Not strong enough.
Aren't grateful to live somewhere free.
Somewhere civilized.
We saved you from yourself, Black girl.

We are the living embodiment of generational trauma.
Knowing our aversion to water is because they threw our
babies into lakes as alligator bait.
Because they poured acid into our swimming pools.
Because they tried to extinguish our flame existence with
fire hoses.
Because I know my ancestors were raped and killed and I
carry their abusers' last names.

Heavy is the head that wears the crown, and we need laws in
order to wear our crowns naturally.
When they crack batons over our heads and we bleed out and
black out, only then will they call us strong Black women.
Praise us for calm reactions. The broken smiles. The clenched
fists.
They will rave about how we handled the abuse so well.
Because we can not crack, we can not flinch, so we smile.

Because Black girls aren't grappling with suicide.
Don't question our worth in this life.
Don't fantasize about the stillness death might bring.

Wouldn't want people thinking you're sick, Black girl.
To think you're mentally ill, Black girl.
Might think you're crazy, Black girl.
And you know what we do to women who are "crazy."
We lock them up.
Lobotomize them.

Stigmatize them.
So you better not look like you need help, Black girl.

So we cover the cracks in our mental health with "I'm fine."
Suffer in silence.
Conflate depression and anxiety with failing.
Act as if centuries of oppression don't make you lose your shit.
Act as if knowing our history doesn't affect our mental health.
Act as if generational trauma is not a form of PTSD.
Act as if anxiety doesn't cripple my body every time I see a cop car.

We can't crack, so we smile.

I am tired of holding up this crumbling foundation.

I am angry.

I am sad.

I am unwell.

Never hide the scars and the disjointed pieces, they are beautiful and real.
Our cracks are not imperfections, not something to be disguised or fixed.

I am blessed by the brokenness, so I will crack, I will shatter.
Our emotions are valid, Black girl.
We have every right to be angry, Black girl.
Our mental health is everything, Black girl.
You are everything, Black girl.

This poem was created for a dance class for older adults through Ormao Dance Company. The themes of this class were "how we come together, memory (personal and collective), and the quilt as a metaphor for a community that honors differences." As the participants danced, they spoke a few lines from this poem.

Remember

Remember who you are.
All that you came from and the earth that birthed you.
Trace generations along the lines of upturned palms offering connection to the hands of our neighbors.
We are never far from those who walked before us.
Memories wrapped in senses tell stories of ourselves and our lineage.
Feel the embrace of a loved one holding the stress we carry.
Release shoulders away from ears and breathe into the comfort of connection.
Smell the spices and aromas from cooks making feasts out of leftovers.
Hear the homecoming of languages returning to mother tongues.
See communities coming together to care for each other.
Bring your heart and I'll bring my soul and we'll meet in the seams of a patchwork quilt.
A menagerie of memories connecting the collective and the personal.

The sacred art of fusing beauty, joy, and struggles we each possess to strengthen our resolve.

The stitching, imperfections, and frayed edges are part of the way we honor showing up as human, as people trying their best.

This quilt is a shield.

Protection from cold nights and colder systems.

May we find warmth beneath a creation of our own.

May we never forget who we are, where we came from, and all that we will become.

This was my second Women of Influence award commission. This is a reminder of how proud a person's younger self would be of them. I imagined my younger self meeting me and thinking how cool I was. She would be so surprised I have tattoos and piercings, and proud that I'm a therapist and a poet. I wanted to capture the small things as well as the big accomplishments that our younger selves would be excited to know. This was a healing poem for me, and I hope it offers the same connection and warmth to those who read it.

If She Could See You Now

Remember when this was just a thought or a dream?
When who you've become was a secret you kept under bed frames in an old shoebox.
A declaration you announced willingly to anyone who asked.
Remember when your younger self wondered who you would become?

If she could see you now, there is no limit to the joy you'd bring her.
Happiness rises across her face like an eager sunrise.
She will explore endless possibilities of your excellence.
Brag about all the way she grew into this woman.
She'd list your accomplishments like medieval scrolls dancing along pavement, unrolling softly, telling your whole life story.
Wind chime voice singing your praises.
Diligently accounting for every success, down to getting out of bed each day. She knows this is often the hardest thing to do.

She will give a standing ovation for your body and the adornments.

Trace curious fingers over parts of your body you once thought inadequate and name them treasures.

Celebrate the scars you share and the ones to come.

Revel in the ink and metal you chose as decoration she thought she'd never have.

She will sit in awe of unparalleled beauty and confidence.

She will know her features, her interests, her skin, her hair, her identity are valid.

She'll wonder how someone can stand as tall as forest walls and emit sunbeams of warmth between strong limbs.

She will realize she too is made of sunshine and bark.

She will think you are impossible.

Believe you can do the impossible.

She will ask where your footsteps have traveled.

Realize she will be part of marches, adventures, and revolutions.

She will see that it does get better. Learn it does not get easier.

Take solace knowing you don't know what you're doing.

How you still feel like her, young and curious.

She'll read you as a novel of growth.

Thumb through chapters of struggle and pain and earmark pages where you emerge heroic.

She will wonder if there is still grief in your heart.

Want to add to the alters you've constructed.

Cry alongside you and bear witness to your pain.

Wonder if your dreams found a way outside of closed eyes.

Wonder if you still roll sadness in between your thumb and middle finger, hoping to mold it into motivation.

She will think you are the coolest person in the world.

She will laugh at all of your jokes.

Make playlists of the songs that have taken root in your bones.

Your presence will save her.

You will show her the doors you walked through and ones left closed.

You'll be the answer to a question she was afraid to ask.

You are a love letter to your younger self.
She will read you over and over again.
She will survive knowing you are what's ahead of her.
She is proud of you.
She is rooting for you.
She is you.

Do you remember how far you've come?
Do you know you are the woman your younger self is proud
to be?

As a therapist and someone who provides care to caregivers in the healthcare field, I see my work as helping to carry the heavy weights we all hold. When we shift that weight, we can reach higher and feel lighter.

Rise

We rise by lifting others.
Making weightless our mosaic bodies when we feel tethered to our distress.
Tangled in grief.
Strapped down by exhaustion.
Barricaded by frustration.
Let us hold what you've been carrying.
Practice setting down and letting go.
Untangling and liberating from things that have gone unsaid.
Exchange guilt and shame for kindness and validation.

See us drop sandbag struggle, worried weights, and watch us rise.
Scream until your voice catches on the wind and creates change.
Commune with others who have shared your experiences and watch us rise in connection to our community.
Let the fire of your passions grow and lift us with each act of activism.

We rise from the inside out.
We are standing with you, rising alongside you, making buoy-
ant this institution.
This work is bidirectional.
We are saving each other every time we reach out to each other.

Every time you feel seen, we rise.
Every act of self-care you implement, we rise.
When you experience joy, we rise.
When you know you are not alone in this world, we rise.

The sky is not expansive enough for this journey.
Our healing is not limited to this atmosphere.
We will rise as long as there is a need to heal.
We will rise as high as our connection takes us.
We cannot rise without you.
We remain here for you, to lift and be lifted by each other.

Working as a therapist and caring for hospital workers during Covid was painful, fulfilling, and difficult. This poem showcases how our work saved lives, but it also took, and continues to take, a toll on our physical and mental health. We came together in this critical time of need, and we all deserve to exhale and release from the past few years of the pandemic.

Exhale

As a child, I played a game where I held my breath when driving through a tunnel.
If I could hold it until the end, it was good luck and I could make a wish.
As we reflect on the past year, I notice many of us have been holding our breath, hoping we can make it to the end and wish for something new.

We began holding our breath for the safety of our patients, coworkers, families, and communities.
Holding our breath while holding up the foundations of our lives.
In response, we made life preserves out of our eye contact, grew community gardens of grace, and reinforced humanity and support from six feet away.
We were exhausted, scared, and anxious, but we kept going.

We held our breath as our way of life shifted rapidly.
We held our breath during calls for justice and social unrest.

We held our breath as our children navigated school in various forms.
We held our breath as we grieved loved ones from a distance.
We held our breath when we didn't know what else to do.

There was sacrifice, tears, pain, and even joy.
We learned it was okay to not know the answers and to admit the complexities and difficulties of existing each day.
We fell softly into the care of our mental and physical health.
We leaned on each other and created a new culture of care.

We saved lives.
The lives of our patients and the lives of our Denver Health family.
We found our way through darkness and uncertainty.
At times the light was dim and far away, but we kept going, waiting for the tunnel to come to an end.
We became a beacon of hope, realizing each of us possessed a light. We illuminated the darkness to reveal we were never alone. We've been finding our way through it all together.

As we reflect on this year, may we all exhale.
Release the good luck we've earned from seventeen months of held breath.
Our collective release is community healing.
What we know is that we need each other.
We are finding survival and hope with every sunrise.
Learning to breathe again, without fear, as we move forward through the tunnel.
Acknowledging the strength and light within us all.

This piece was commissioned for the Colorado Springs Chamber & Economic Development Corporation Gala to highlight businesses and economic development. I am continually inspired by the stars and Orion is one of my favorite constellations. I enjoyed relating aspects of our community to the tools a warrior needs to succeed.

Orion

There are more stars in the universe than grains of sand on all the beaches on earth.
With roughly 10 sextillion grains of sand and about 200 sextillion stars, there is no comparison.
The night sky holds a universe of light, energy, and guidance not unlike our community.
A collection of diverse stars across storied history coming together in formation.
We are a constellation.
Orion is one of the brightest and most known constellations.
Containing 2 of the 10 brightest stars in the sky.
Marked by a hunter with a shield and hand raised high. Defined by three stars as a belt.
See us in this depiction of strength, power, and beauty.

Small businesses sharing their passion and skill make up the shield. Forming connected networks that fortify the economy. We cannot win the battle without them.

The hand raised in revolution and liberation holds a variety of industries. Creating community impact, jobs, development, and advancement.

Businesses are the armor adorning our city with the tools to persevere and build a better future.

The body is intersectional.
The body is made of women in leadership mentoring others to become CEOs and directors in STEM fields.
The body is BIPOC business owners and directors redefining historical norms and professions.
The body recognizes visible and invisible identities and fights for accessibility through advancements in technology.
The body honors and protects gender and sexuality.
The body knows being authentic paves the way for new opportunities.

We need all of us in this constellation.
Every star and every business is unique and integral to the structure of this city
The three-star belt is diversity, equity, and inclusion.
Guiding the will to stand up for and with all of our neighbors.
This trio is our reminder of what drives us, that a seat at the table is no longer enough.
It is what we do once at the table that matters.
When all voices are lifted up and integrated into decisions, there is no battle Orion can't win.
The fight in Orion is akin to our resilience.
Resilience is not a character trait we earn, it is a power deep within us to battle until sunrise.
As the night fades and our starlight bodies are lifted by the warming sun.
We rest. We heal. We prepare once again to add our story to the constellation.

In Sumerian mythology the name Orion means "the light of heaven," and aren't we a light.
A collection of each of our histories, resilience, identity, and passion.
Making this city one of the brightest stars in Colorado.

I am intrigued by the rich Black history in my city, Colorado Springs. Most of the Black history I've found has been through my own research, and hardly anything was taught in school. The book The Invisible People of the Pikes Peak Region by John Holley is dedicated to Black history in the Springs, and it highlights people and places who have contributed to the city. I have a poem published in the reprint of this book, and I have spent many hours reading and learning about our history. I worked with the Pioneers Museum for Black History Month to select Black historical sites and people, then created poems to tell their stories. This piece is about the first Black church in Colorado Springs, Carter Payne. Black churches have always been a hub and haven for connection, food drives, volunteer work, activism, and more. This piece is about the Carter Payne Chapel, but I believe it applies to all Black churches and their presence in the Black community. I also believe it's important to express that some Black churches have also had a hand in harming their congregants, especially those in the queer community. This piece examines the foundations of having a space just for Black people, which helped many survive in communities and cities that were actively trying to drive them out.

An Ode to a Black Church

How many lives have you saved?
Become home and hideout.
Sanctuary after a week of the world trying to take your spirit.
Trying to convince you this city wasn't built for us.
Sunday as a reset, as a catalyst for renewed resilience.
A place of holiness where God looks like us. Created us in his image.
A congregation of beautiful Black people of Colorado Springs.
This chapel was a sacred space where we could gather as free people, as God's people.
Where prayers collected at the top of the church and escaped to heaven when the doors let out.
Bodies bouncing and swaying. Praising and worshiping.

Hallelujah and amen served as a siren song to call home those looking for belonging.

Before there was donated land from General Palmer and Bear Creek brick, church was where two or more were gathered in his midst and were blessed.
Homes were the only places to convene when other churches didn't recognize melanin as a gift of divinity.
Wouldn't allow us to darken their steps.
But supremacy has never stopped the Black community from caring for each other, for practicing ritual and religion.
The Carter brothers opened their residence and made space for others to feel at home, to feel saved.
Black churches have always been spaces of our own.
Centralizing the Black community.
Sites for activism and leadership, food distribution, housing, and filling community needs.
I know the Carter Payne Chapel has saved lives.
Created a safe haven so Blackness could breathe and thrive for generations to come, for generations to know they are always welcome.
Although the time came to transition out of a spiritual meeting space, the structure will always be a landmark of the first Black Church in Colorado Springs.
A legacy of Black History.

This poem is the product of my first art residency! I worked with the Green Box Arts Festival to create a poem for the newly installed James Turrell Skyspace in Green Mountain Falls. During my residency, I got the chance to experience the sunrise showing in the Skyspace and became the first non-staff person to see the full showing at this location. I was picked up from my artist's apartment at around 4:30 a.m. by three men in a truck. We made our way up the winding road to the Skyspace tucked into the mountainside, and I had a truly beautiful experience. I drew on the story of the allegory of the cave for this piece, as the experience breaks the rules of light and color and challenges our reality. I wanted this poem to be a call to action to encourage others to visit the space and see a new reality. I encourage you to take a trip to Green Mountain Falls and visit the Skyspace to get the full experience of this poem.

Look Up

I dare you to lock up in the Skyspace.
Embrace a new perspective.
Live fully in the present moment.
Ceremonially disrobe your preconceived notions.
Leave them at the door and walk into curiosity.
Turn your head toward a universe aching to connect.
Lock eyes with studded stars and beveled clouds.
Ground feet on smooth tile, lean back, and formally introduce
yourself to the world existing right above us.
Stare boldly into a piece of sky carved out of the collective
unconscious.
Tuck away the secrets you learn, scribed in the apex sunrise.
Honor the wisdom brush-stroked across sunset nights.
Nourish the soul in Technicolor brilliance.
Experience the way light alters our perception.
Catalyst colors turn night skies bright blue with the softness
of an inhale.

Watch the world transform before your eyes.
Marvel at your eyes transforming reality before you.
Build it without ever saying a word
The silence is not the absence of sound but the stillness of spirit.
Your spirit deserves to rest.
Heal in this space.
Collectively feel what it means to dream without limits.
Emerge after the colors have danced along walls and washed over you.
Travel down the worn path back to what we thought we knew.
Invite those who have yet dared to dream to step into the artistry of their imagination.
Share how the sky is a canvas and we are Impressionists.
Painting joy with an exhale.
Fostering healing in a blink of an eye.
I dare you to look up and imagine a world of your own.

Philanthropy has always been a huge part of my life. After college, I was a fellow with the El Pomar Foundation, and I went on to become the program director of an art nonprofit. I was asked to create a poem for the 315 Philanthropy Collective, an innovative look at foundations. Foundations from across Colorado moved their offices into a shared space to collaboration and create a larger impact the region. The Well is the restaurant connected to the building. It supports the foundation and provides more opportunities to connect over food and drink. I loved translating the power of philanthropy and shared meals in the poem. The driving theme for this piece was the phrase "better together."

Better Together

Philanthropy is not defined by the sum of the gift, but by the capacity with which there is love for humanity.

Imagine one gift.

One act of good.

One show of investment.

How it can ripple through a community like a smooth skipped stone and reinvigorate its environment.

This is the impact of one.

We are in the business of many.

The coming together of minds, hearts, and passionate givers, in the pursuit of revolutionary actions by which we multiply the love of humanity and the care of our neighbors.

So we may continue to thrive, envision a just and equitable future, and add to the brilliance of our home.

The practice is simple and the ritual is sacred.

The gathering under one roof.

The pooling of resources to amass a wealth of opportunities to impact the region.

The affirmation that we can do more and be better together, for good.

Listening and amplifying the voices of identities once silenced, but always present.

It is the breaking of bread and relational healing.

Creating a gathering place for souls to nourish and rest alongside the active work.

It is the metronome of trust and integrity guiding us, and the devotion to our community that will sustain us.

We are the first to practice in this way.

To embody and acknowledge we are better together as healers, funders, and community members.

Forging a ritual that others can follow.

Grounding this practice as foundational to the work and the region.

No longer are we a single rock aimed to impact an ocean at the surface level.

We are a seismic event.

We are conscious and collective vibrations that will change the landscape from within.

We are wavemakers.

Unstoppable and dynamic potential beginning to crest.

This is the start of a legacy.

This is the love of the Pikes Peak Region.

These are the questions I've asked myself across my lifetime and through my experiences in toxic and abusive relationships and situations. These are the questions friends, clients, and colleagues have asked during and after their experiences. This is real. It's the unfortunate reality and fear of not being believed. This poem was created for a local domestic violence organization.

Break the Silence

How do you tell someone your trauma, when they will think you asked for it?
When you willingly went home with him, dated him, married him, and walked away feeling like you left pieces of your body across the years.
How do you ask for support when you enjoyed the majority of his body, but didn't ask for the last two minutes?
What stories will they write about you when he puts his hands on your neck to choke you in the midst of making love, thinking consent to being inside your body means consent to all of your body?

How do you explain a violation that was preceded by consent?
Where do you find safety when the first no to his attempt was met with force and you answered yes in fear of him taking want he wanted?
What number do you call when he grabs you in your home and forces you to kiss him?

How do you report the robbery of your body, when you let him in and gave him access to valuables?
Who do you ask for help when he doesn't leave marks on your skin?
When he strangles your self-esteem, punches your emotions until they submit, and cuts off your supply of support?
What police reports do you file when there is no evidence of abuse?
When he is a nice guy.
When the nice guy knows how to be a good guy in front of the public.

Who will believe you when you start to second-guess yourself?
Who will affirm you when you are the only one who thinks you were hurt, and your memory refuses to release the photographic evidence?
What church do you run to when you can't keep track of the times you prayed he would die to make it easier for you to leave?
Who will come for you after you tell them it wasn't that bad?
How do you save yourself after you say it wasn't that bad?
When you think at least he didn't rape me, punch me, assault me, kill me.
At least I can write this poem about it. I made it out alive, and there are others who didn't have the chance.
At least it wasn't as bad as . . .
He's a better person now so . . .
He doesn't even remember when . . .
He didn't leave a scar . . .

There is no excuse big enough to invalidate your experience.
No reputation powerful enough to discredit your name.
There is no statute of limitations on your story.
When you ever question how or who or why.
Know your voice will always break the silence, and we're here to listen.

October is Arts Month, and I was asked to create a poem for the Arts Month proclamations to share with City Council and the county commissioners. I wanted to represent various forms of art and highlight all the ways art makes our community a better place. I conceptualize this as a blessing.

Arts Month Proclamation

Art is a proclamation of our radiant souls creating unapologetically.
Building bridges from tongues disenfranchised to hearts ready to listen
Art is no longer just entertainment.
It is a modality for healing.
A sacred ritual.
A conversation with the community
Our artists are the translators of what adds to the beauty of our region.

Blessed are the poets.
Writers with pens posed to capture fleeting moments.
Spinning stories grand and epic, to be remembered forever.
They will find beauty in the mundane details of life.
Turn the changing of the leaves into an odyssey of letting go and transitions.
Capturing history in metaphors so we may never lose sight of our beginnings.

Adding meaning when we need it the most.
Tetrising syntax for poetic beauty.

Blessed are the painters.
Brushstroke brilliance.
Visionaries of this land, depict us in ways where we fall in love with ourselves.
Cartographer of community cohesion.
Capturing the abstract, the complex, and the joyous in pencil, chalk, clay, or metal.
Inspire a dedication to the process.
How it's impossible to stay clean when creating, and recognizing the mess is a part of the art.
They will show us what a better world looks like, textured, and dynamic.

Blessed are the musicians.
Symphonic demonstrations of creative chaos.
Soundtrack humanity's exploration of ourselves.
Create a sensory experience that vibrates our souls.
Amplify the marginalized, bring their voices high, surrounded by an accompaniment of validation.
Honor the offbeats, the melodies, the rap lyrics.
Teach us that harmony sounds like yelling, crying, breathing, and laughing.
It sounds like authentic self-expression.
Conduct us in grace and support of our neighbors.

Blessed are the dancers.
Calligraphy in motion.
Sharing drama, tragedy, and love, all with a pointed toe.
Move the hurt through with fluidity.
They will help us reclaim our bodies.
Move back into our hearts and minds and make a home.
Teach us to move without judgment and give ourselves over to the experiences of radical joy.

Blessed are the actors.
They will decolonize our movements.
Teach us the Theater of the Oppressed.
Guide us in rituals.
Utilize our bodies to give thanks and reverence.
Teach us how to store blessings more than we do trauma.
They will help us take off our masks.
The actors will reveal the ways our world is all a stage.
Allow us space to take a bow and shed our disguises for the good of the people and the good of ourselves.
Remind us of the emotions we've forgotten we can feel.
Act out our fantasies, dreams, and pains so we may heal.

Blessed are the comedians.
Bubbling laughter in bellies and willing it to escape in vibrancy.
Alchemy pain and loss into jokes that aim to heal.
We laugh so we do not cry.
They teach us to laugh until we cry.
They will lead a revolution of tight cheeks, wild smiles, and delight.
May we shelter ourselves in the collective giggles, chortles, and chuckles.

We are a blank canvas.
Full of possibilities and potential
Let this month be the invitation for the artists to create.
To get messy.
To pour into our community and fill every inch of empty space.
Paint the edges.
Collaborate and collage artistic endeavors.
Record the sounds of artists at work, and dance to it. Paint to it. Dream to it.
This is an invitation to reap the benefits of creativity bridging new perspectives.
May we loudly, enthusiastically, and in community, celebrate the arts.

Panorama Park is a community park in the southeast of Colorado Springs. The southeast is a largely Black and Brown community. Prior to the renovation, this park didn't represent the beauty of the neighborhood. It was a huge milestone for the city as organizations came together to revamp the park with a playground, bike path, exercise equipment, stage, and more. I had the amazing opportunity to sit down with folks on the planning committee as well as community members. I learned about the community's connection to the park and created a poem inviting them to play there, reinforcing that it represents their already powerful community. I took the perspective of a meeting place. This park is now a place where folks can meet to play, dream, picnic, and relax. My job with this poem was to let people know the park is theirs and that we are excited and eager for them to use it.

Panorama Park

Meet me at Panorama Park, where our stories have taken root and birthed the community.
Feel the transfer of wisdom, ingenuity, and dedication as you enter and explore.
Built on the foundation that joy is our birthright.

Meet me in the place where you can go to reconvene with your breath.
Find stillness even amongst a breeze.
Soak in an unmatched view and let a smile sunrise across your face as the radiance of the Rocky Mountains meets your gaze.

Meet me in the place where we gather in love and light.
A once desolate land now reinvigorated by the passion of the people.
We did not fix a community nor give it something it never had.
We shined a light on the heart of the southeast of Colorado Springs.

Modeled the beautification of this space after the soul of the people.
Representing that we have always been here.
Vibrant and diverse.
Existing and thriving.

Meet me in the place where if you listen, you can hear whispers in the wind.
This park is a collective voice that has gathered strength from decades of advocacy and leadership.
Pulling from youth, organizations, elders, and citizens in collaboration.
Harmonizing needs and visions that have become an anthem.
Can you hear them?
They are saying, "Step into your power."
Recognize we have always been the source of the light.
Resilience lives inside all of us.
The hard work was excavating preconceived notions and barriers.
Creating an unprecedented project for progress.
Making way for a destination that belongs to each of us.
A culmination of legacies in motion and fortified.

This is collective work, but we are not finished.
We need you to play.
Use imagination on open fields and jungle gyms.
Pick up basketball games and leave everything on the court.
Experience joy with abandon.

We need you to adventure.
Ride bikes and skateboards on winding paths.
Run hands across tile art and feel the connection to others.
Exercise and move your body.

We need you to dream.
Find yourself in the shade next to loved ones.

Create poetic magic in the presence of nature.
Fantasize about ideas that will change the world.

Explore here.
Play here.
Heal here.

Meet me at the place you are proud to call your own.
Where you fully know you are enough.
Deserving of elation and jubilation.
Where change no longer feels unreachable.
Where community is active and flourishing.
Where your voice is heard.

Meet me at Panorama Park.

Arts Vision 2030 was a committee tasked to create the ten-year artistic plan for Colorado Springs. As committee members, we developed goals and a vision for our community as it relates to the arts. I was asked to create a poem to include with the ten-year plan, which embodies all of our goals and engages the community with our arts vision.

The Time Is Now

Now is the time to be bold!
Surrender fear to the exploration of new creative endeavors.

Now is the time to be courageous!
Advocate for each other loudly and without hesitation.

Now is the time to be collaborative!
We are at our strongest when we connect, share, and champion each other.

Now is the time to be innovative!
Reimagine art with accessibility and equity across the region.

Now is the time to lead with change!
Art is a catalyst for revolution, liberation, and progression.

Now is the time to create art in the image of our region!
Where every person can say, "I am reflected in the art I see in my community."

This is the future we are working toward.
Art representing your neighborhood, family, identity, heritage, passions, pain, and joys.
Art weaving into the fabric of the region seamlessly.
Art permeating systems, institutions, and structures of power.

To leaders, teachers, artists, and community members, your voice matters.
From BIPOC, queer, disabled, women, and other marginalized groups, your voice matters.
Your voice and the voices of our diverse community are integral to this vision.
The uplifting and collective support of each other is the only way through.
It will take all of us to implement this work.
We cannot do this without you.
We need you to champion art in the ways only you can.

See yourself reflected in these declarations.
Make your home in the words and be held by their support.
Feel the way your body is called to a specific action.
Find the ways you add to the vibrance of art and creativity in this vision, and join us.
Fight alongside us to be better tomorrow than we are today.
We see our future for art as lifesaving.
We see the future of art in you.

Let art become aspen grove.
An interconnected network of roots that supply and nourish each other.
Despite size or range, let us come together for the good of the people.
Stand in solidarity and community with those similar and different from yourself.
Bound by creativity and possibilities.
As we grow the legacy of art in the Pikes Peak Region.

Theatreworks put on the production of The Bluest Eye directed by Lynne Hastings, written by Toni Morrison and adapted by Lydia R. Diamond. I was honored to be involved in organizing a spoken word collaboration. I have worked with Theatreworks in the past, putting together poetry readings alongside their plays or curating artists for talk-backs. I had the incredible privilege of curating poets for the talkback for this production. The Bluest Eye is an intense book and play focusing on Black trauma through a powerful metaphor, and it was an instrumental book in my life. For many theater experiences in Colorado Springs, the typical patrons are not part of the BIPOC community. I wanted there to be a bridge between The Bluest Eye, a fictional story about the Black experience, and the real experiences of the Black arts community and how the two interacted. I pitched the idea to have poets perform a piece about The Bluest Eye at the close of the play to provide perspective and demonstrate how instrumental this book has been to so many Black people. This was my submission for the production.

Trinity

Blonde hair, blue eyes, white skin.

Blonde hair, blue eyes, white skin.

Blonde hair, blue eyes, white skin.

Beauty began with lunchroom comments about never dating a Black girl and the superiority of every feature I didn't have.

Anger began when I was told to sit at the back of the bus during a field trip, and called Ebony and Ivory when standing next to my friend.

Hatred began when White boys in elementary school wouldn't touch me so my Black wouldn't rub off on them.

Ugly began when I was the only Black girl in my class for years and didn't have at least one of the holy three.

The sacred trinity.

If not all, then at least one. Give me one so I can survive, so I can uncloak myself and be seen. Just one, so I may exist and have protection on school buses, in lunch rooms, and in classrooms. I'm only asking for one, to bring me closer to what the world tells me I am lacking.

Let me be beautiful, let me be good. Just one and maybe I could love the mirror and the image. Maybe the body will heal from brick-laced comments. Maybe my skin won't tighten and stretch itself thin to be invisible. Just one is all I need.

God never answered. Never gave me at least one. I spent young years thinking I wasn't enough to receive. Believed a God who looked like them and not like me wouldn't turn to face my siren calls.

I know now I was asking for something I didn't need. I was already full of divine creation. I was a masterpiece of design.

Black girls are twilight moonscapes and tidal-wave sunsets.
We run hands through hair and find magic on our fingertips.
Wide noses and high cheekbones situate our beauty on mountaintop landscapes.
Bodies, vessels of dreams come true with our existence.
Dear Black girls, never look back to beauty standards too fragile to house Blackness, too narrow to celebrate how melanin velvets our skin.

Our bodies are reclamation.
Do not let them dispossess us of ourselves.
Every time a Black girl falls in love with herself she saves a life.

See clearly with the eyes of the beholder that we are everything we have been looking for.

We are marigolds
Thriving in hours of sunlight to produce a trinity of our own.
Joy, bright as sunbeams cresting from our smiles into the warm yellow petals.
Confidence, sprawling into purple royalty and straightening our backs and lifting our chins.
Grace, to love ourselves in full bloom, wrapped in loud expressions of green.

We are the soil, the trunk, the fruit, and the bloom.

Black girls, we have arrived at ourselves and to a God that looks like us.
Dripping out of full lips with dialects and twangs, we say,

Brown hair, brown eyes, brown skin.

Brown hair, brown eyes, brown skin.

Brown hair, brown eyes, brown skin.

A trinity of beauty unlike any other.

Inside Out Youth Services is an incredible organization serving LGBTQIA2+ youth in Colorado Springs. Inside Out has a special place in my heart, and I have had the honor to work with the youth, doing poetry in a variety of ways over the years. I was invited to the staff retreat and worked with Inside Out staff. I hosted a poetry workshop, and throughout the session, I gathered some of the staff's phrasing and quotes and created a poem at the end of the workshop. This is the culmination of my work with Inside Out employees, and it bears witness to their heart, passion, and drive.

Inside Out

We provide space for firework hearts and rivers of expression.
Replace shame with revolutionary celebration.

Our cups are filled with joy.
The joy of release and elation and the joy of naming the complex parts.

Watch as we shed and are reborn in light.
May our collective healing leave seeds along our path and birth inspiration.
Our existence is saving lives.

Watch us close our eyes in rest.
Claim it for those forced away.

Copy our dedication to me, we, you, us.

In community.

In service of ourselves and others.
We commit to radical care, to shouting, to being sledge-hammer loud.

Remembering to hold each other in grace and humanity.

We believe in the work.
We believe in this community.
We believe inside and out of us.

This poem was commissioned by the Laboratory to Combat Human Trafficking. One of the transformative lessons I learned from taking this organization's training was that human traffickers look like your neighbor, your doctor, and your teacher. So often we are looking for "monsters" and missing the real culprits who are standing right in front of us. This poem is a play on "a wolf in sheep's clothing."

Because I Know

We've been told to watch out for wolves in poorly constructed disguises.
The obvious bushy tail poking out of a grandmother's dress.
The pointed claws of an unusually tall sheep, or citrine eyes behind tiny reading glasses.

We've been told it's easy to spot the bad guys, the evil, the menacing.
Taught to underestimate the sophistication of a wolf on the hunt.
How hiding in plain sight is the easiest way to operate, until we learned wolves are not anthropomorphic concepts of the bad.
Not traps of sharp snarling fangs or alleyways darkened by shadowed figures.
But instead, the wolf hides in between the teeth of a warm smile.
Nestles itself in the corners we rarely turn to face.
Making invisible those walking unchained but unable to leave.

When you are expecting a monster, you can forget to look at man.

Society silenced survivors long before the traffickers did.

Because we were told we weren't looking in the right places.

When in reality we were looking into the faces in the right places.

Not realizing that the dishwasher hidden in the back of the restaurant who isn't allowed to leave or contact his family is trafficked.

The migrant worker trying to pay off their debt in an attempt for a better life, working twelve-hour days in ninety-degree weather with no breaks or water, is trafficked.

The trans youth kicked out of their house, trying to find family and safety working in a motel, is trafficked.

The young boy being forced into sexually abusive situations, afraid that if he leaves, his family will be in danger, is trafficked.

The mother who fell in love with a man who said he'd take care of her and her kids, then forced her to work for him and stole their IDs and phones, is trafficked.

This is the unmasking.

The humanizing.

The education.

The reckoning that human trafficking impacts all people, all ages, races, genders, sexualities, classes, and lived experiences.

Trafficking is forced labor. Is debt bondage. Is sex.

Because we know how wolves hide themselves, we can find those stuck in their teeth.

Dislodge them from lockjaw confinement.

We can change invisibility to deep intentionality.

Notice when your intuition sparks curiosity.

Report and save a life.

Get trained to correct the stereotypes and spread knowledge.

Donate and give your heart and treasure to those in need.

Support survivors.

Become a conscious consumer.
Commit the revolutionary act of caring for another person.
Release the voices ensnared in the throats of wolves.
Allow them to share their stories.
Remind those taught to be wary of wolves in sheep's clothing
that the wolves should be afraid of what we know.

I had the incredible opportunity to create a poem and perform it for the opening of Valarie Kaur's keynote address at La Foret Conference & Retreat Center. I was inspired by Valarie's work and wanted to capture how the act of revolutionary love will change the future. As a poet, poetry is how I understand the revolution and blending these two ideas together created this beautiful piece.

Revolutionary Love

The revolution will be poetic.
Full of voices waxing and waning on the beauty of the future.
Lyrical lamentations decorating time. Marking historic events in melodic form.

Injustice will be hyperbole, something overstated and unimaginable. Only realized in works of fiction.

Every person is a neighbor in homes built from the concretized prayers of our ancestors. Guided by affirmations honoring our most deep-rooted needs.

There are no strangers here. The sweet sonnet of our name lives as a collective unconscious.
A reminder that we have always been a part of each other.

The revolution is the coming back to one another from mother tongues, sacred religions, and honored traditions and reuniting with humanity.

There will be odes to melanin, queerness, disability, and all that once was marginalized.

Our productivity will be measured by how much rest and joy we get each day. Pleasure is a quota we eagerly aim for, an epic journey of perpetuity.

We honor our pain as true and real. The grief we possess never gets smaller, but we grow in our capacity to hold it, integrate it into our being.

May we link arms with others who have hurt and create a container for our collective healing. Become a lighthouse for others wading in darkness believing they are lost. Until they bump into our interconnected network and rediscover their light.

The revolution will reimagine systems.
Schools will be generational storytelling hubs. Oral history dismantling White supremacy.
Museums will be empty and treasured relics and artifacts returned to those once stolen.

We will come back to bodies once stolen and create treasure maps for others to follow back to themselves.
We will free fall in love with ourselves. In doing so drop the weighted burdens of learned hate and watch them dissipate.

We have been resisting for so long we've forgotten that fighting isn't the only way to win.
The revolution is the release, the exhale, the softening into, and the rebirth.
Creation outside of oppression.
A decolonized landscape fertile with imagination, where resilience is not the consequence of violence or trauma, but an expression of brilliancy and motivation.

Love is the only way through, a catalyst for the return to wonder.
A daily intentional practice to labor for ourselves, others, and our opponents.
To meet in the middle and daydream in poetic verse.
Make our language and form a manifesto of revolutionary love.

I created this poem for Kaiser's Black History Month celebration. The phrase "We are our ancestors' wildest dreams" comes up all the time; in fact, it comes up a lot in this book. I imagine their dreams were not about productivity or working, but about safety, joy, rest, and love. I know my ancestors just want me to lie down and take a break. This poem is a comfort and a reminder to slow down, a reminder that joy is more important than work!

Our Ancestors Dreamed of Rest

Black people are innovators, educators, doctors, artists, and so much more.
We are built into the foundations of this country through our accomplishments and contributions.
Our influence is seen from the smallest act to the largest system.
Black excellence is more than our productivity.
We are first and foremost people who experience rest and joy.
We are our ancestors' wildest dreams.
A turn of phrase draping us in gratitude for our existence.
But what they dreamed of was not continued work.
They dreamed we would rest without fear.
They dreamed of laughter, connection, and celebration.
They dreamed we would know joy, returning to embrace it over and over again.

We are a collection of sacred prayers realized in our Black experience.
Every time we experience joy, we are acting in revolution.

Centering our pleasure is a protest of confinement.

Excellence is existing and thriving in spaces that never expected us to gain access.

Excellence is taking care of our mental health and honoring our emotions.

Excellence is the way our creativity influences all aspects of our society.

Excellence is in the recognition of each other.

Of the head nods down hallways, in grocery stores, and sidewalks.

We see each other like no one else can.

We see our beauty in Technicolor melanin.

We hear love in accents, dialects, and slang.

We feel warmth when we occupy space together.

We are a visceral experience.

To some, excellence is measured by what we have added to this world.

But we know excellence is rooted in ancestral connection to rest and joy.

This is our birthright.

This is our inheritance.

Acknowledgments

I would like to express my heartfelt gratitude to all those who have supported and encouraged me throughout the writing and publishing of my first poetry book.

Special thanks to my family, partner, and friends for their constant belief in my artistic expression and encouragement.

I would also like to thank God and my ancestors for the continuous blessings, wisdom, and unconditional love.

To my readers, thank you for taking the time to explore my words and connect with the translations from my soul expressed in this book. Your support means the world to me.

Thank you to all of the organizations, businesses, and individuals who have hired me for commissioned work and believed in the power of my words.

Thank you to the Black, BIPOC, Queer, and Art communities of Colorado Springs and Denver, who have empowered and uplifted my voice.

Lastly, a huge thank you to the publishers and everyone else involved in bringing this book to life. Your hard work and dedication have made this dream a reality.

Thank you all from the bottom of my heart.

ABOUT THE AUTHOR

Ashley Cornelius is the 6th Pikes Peak Region Poet Laureate based in Colorado Springs, Colorado. Ashley is the youngest and the first Black person to hold this title. Ashley is a multi-award winning spoken word poet, keynote speaker, workshop facilitator, and community organizer. Ashley is a Licensed Professional Counselor and utilized poetry therapy interventions as her modality for healing. Ashley is the Co-Director of Poetry719, a Black-led grassroots poetry movement that was created out of the necessity for dedicated art spaces for marginalized communities and their artistic self-expression. Ashley is committed to using poetry as a platform to speak up and out for marginalized groups and be a voice for those who have been historically silenced.

To learn more about Ashley and her work:

 Instagram: @accpoetrynow

 Website: www.ashleycornelius.com

Journey Institute Press

Journey Institute Press is a non-profit publishing house created by authors to flip the publishing model for new authors. Created with intention and purpose to provide the highest quality publishing resources available to authors whose stories might otherwise not be told.

JI Press focusses on women, BIPOC, and LGBTQ+ authors without regard to the genre of their work.

As a Publishing House, our goal is to create a supportive, nurturing, and encouraging environment that puts the author above the publisher in the publishing model.

Wordbinders Publishing is an Imprint of Journey Institute Press, a division of 50 in 52 Journey, Inc.

One final note. The world of publishing has changed dramatically. This has also affected authors and their ability to let readers know about their books. Most people buy books based on word of mouth these days.

If you have the time and would like to help this author, please consider leaving an honest review of this book on retail sites and book community sites such as Goodreads.